The Dominican Tradition

Phyllis Zagano

Thomas C. McGonigle, O.P.

LITURGICAL PRESS
Collegeville, Minnesota

www.litpress.org

Cover design by Ann Blattner. Cover art: Fra Angelico, *Saint Dominic Contemplating the Scriptures,* c. 1438.

1   2   3   4   5   6   7   8   9

Library of Congress Cataloging-in-Publication Data

Zagano, Phyllis.
    The Dominican tradition / Phyllis Zagano, Thomas C. McGonigle.
        p.   cm. — (Spirituality in history series)
    Includes bibliographical references.
    ISBN-13: 978-0-8146-1911-7 (alk. paper)
    ISBN-10: 0-8146-1911-8 (alk. paper)
        1. Dominicans--Spiritual life.   I. McGonigle, Thomas C., 1941–   II. Augustine, Saint, Bishop of Hippo. Regula.   III. Title.   IV. Series.

BX3503.Z36   2006
271'.2—dc22   2006008193

Contents

Acknowledgments

Excerpt from *Saint Dominic: Biographical Documents*, ed. F. C. Lehner, O.P. Washington, DC: The Thomist Press (1964) 91–92, 148–59. Reprinted with permission.

Excerpt by St. Albert the Great is from *Supplement to the Liturgy of the Hours for the Order of Preachers: A Draft Translation of the Proprium Officiorum Ordinis Praedicatorum (1982) for Study and Consultation*. River Forest, Illinois: Dominican Liturgical Commission, U.S.A. (1991) 407–19. Reprinted with permission.

Excerpts from *Compendium of Theology* by Thomas Aquinas are from *Aquinas's Shorter Summa*. Manchester, NH: Sophia Institute Press (1993, 2002). 1-800-888-9344. Reprinted with permission.

Excerpts from *Albert & Thomas: Selected Writings*, from The Classics of Western Spirituality, translated, edited, and introduced by Simon Tugwell, O.P., preface by Leonard E. Boyle, O.P., Copyright © 1988 by Simon Tugwell, O.P., New York/Mahwah, N.J. Used with permission of Paulist Press. www.paulistpress. com.

Excerpts from *Meister Eckhart: Teacher and Preacher*, from The Classics of Western Spirituality, edited by Bernard McGinn, with the collaboration of Frank Tobin and Elvira Borgstadt, preface by Kenneth Northcott, Coypright © 1986 by Bernard McGinn, Paulist Press, Inc., New York/Mahwah, N.J. Used with permission of Paulist Press. www.paulistpress.com.

Excerpts from *Catherine of Siena: The Dialogue*, from The Classics of Western Spirituality, translation and introduction by Suzanne Noffke, O.P., Copyright © 1980 by Paulist Press, Inc., New York/Mahwah, N.J. Used with permission of Paulist Press. www.paulistpress.com.

Excerpt by St. Antoninus Fierozzi is from *Supplement to the Liturgy of the Hours for the Order of Preachers: A Draft Translation of the Proprium Officiorum Ordinis Praedicatorum (1982) for Study and Consultation*. River Forest, Illinois: Dominican Liturgical Commission, U.S.A. (1991) 138–49. All rights reserved. Reprinted with permission.

Preface

The worldwide explosion of interest in "spirituality" has sent inquirers in several directions. One of the more fruitful trajectories is toward the traditional spiritualities that have enriched and nurtured the church for many hundreds of years. Among the oldest Christian spiritualities are those connected to particular foundations, charisms, or individuals. This series on spiritualities in history focuses on five distinct traditions within the history of the church, those now known as Benedictine, Carmelite, Dominican, Franciscan, and Ignatian.

Each volume in the series seeks to present the given spiritual tradition through an anthology of writings by or about persons who have lived it, along with brief biographical introductions of those persons. Each volume is edited by an expert in the tradition at hand.

I have been honored to coedit the present volume of Dominican spirituality with Thomas C. McGonigle, O.P., of the U.S. Province of St. Albert the Great (Central Province), an historian and specialist in the Dominican tradition at Providence College, Rhode Island. Since beginning this project during my tenure as Visiting Aquinas Chair of Catholic Studies at St. Thomas Aquinas College, Sparkill, New York, I have benefited from the generous advice and assistance of a number of other experts in Dominican spirituality and history, including Mary Catherine Hilkert, O.P., University of Notre Dame, and John J. Markey, O.P., U.S. Province of St. Martin de Porres (Southern Province). Several other members of the Dominican family have most generously contributed in large or small ways by supplying materials, discussing particular points, and offering overall good cheer as the book progressed, including Mary de Paul, O.P., Hawthorne; Mary of Jesus, Corpus Christi Monastery, Bronx; Mary Reynolds, O.P., Sparkill; Carleton P. Jones, O.P., of the U.S. Province of St. Joseph (Eastern), New York; Marian McCarthy, o.p., Sinsinawa; Frances Monuszko, o.p., Amityville; Madeleine Murphy, o.p., Sparkill; Virginia Maguire, o.p., Amityville; Gabriel B. O'Donnell, o.p., of the U.S. Province of St. Joseph (Eastern Province), New Haven; Margaret Ormond, o.p., Dominican Sisters International, Rome; and James Sullivan, o.p., of the U.S. Province of St. Joseph (Eastern Province), New York.

Of course no work like this can be completed without the able assistance of librarians, in this case the reference and interlibrary loan staff at Hofstra University, Hempstead, New York, and especially Associate Dean of the Library Paul Glassman; the library staff at Marymount College, Tarrytown, New York, especially Mary Elizabeth Rathgeb, r.s.h.m.; and the librarians at St. Thomas Aquinas College, Sparkill, New York, especially Ken Donohue; and numerous archivists, especially Brinda Frappolo at Rosary Hill Home, Hawthorne, New York, all of whom helped me in this endeavor.

Finally, I acknowledge my indebtedness to all whose professionalism and expertise assisted in this work, especially Ann Blattner, Colleen Stiller, Linda Maloney, Mark Twomey, and Peter Dwyer of the Liturgical Press, and my dear friend Peter J. Houle of New York City.

Phyllis Zagano
October 4, 2005
Feast of St. Francis of Assisi

Introduction

"**D**ominican Spirituality" is at once both easy and impossible to define. It is the lived legacy of St. Dominic's followers, members and affiliates of the Order of Preachers, centered in the mottos associated with the Order: *Laudare, Benedicere, Praedicare.* To praise, to bless, and to preach, from the Preface of the Blessed Virgin Mary in the Roman Missal: *Veritas,* or Truth; and *Contemplare et Contemplata Aliis Tradere,* To contemplate and to hand on the fruits of contemplation. Each motto reflects the core tradition of Dominican life: preaching for the salvation of souls. The many ways by which that core tradition has been understood and lived by Dominicans present a rich tapestry of service to God and God's people.

The lives and writings of the men and women in this volume show how remarkable and dedicated Dominicans over eight centuries have been faithful to St. Dominic's vision, as contemplative preachers in the service of the church in the proclamation of the Gospel. Each represents a different facet of the manifest spirituality of St. Dominic, chosen from among the thousands who have lived that spirituality over the centuries. Those included offer only a snapshot of the whole, without the rich detail that many volumes could present.

The first essay in this book presents a history of the Dominican Tradition and forms the framework and historical background for the individual entries that follow. The life and works of St. Dominic burst forth in the thirteenth century to create a new concept of preaching the gospel, in the vernacular, in and through whatever circumstances arose. St. Dominic's life and preaching drew the first Friars of the Order of Preachers together, and even before he founded the Order for priests and lay brothers, he founded the monastery of Notre Dame de Prouille, with a community of nine women. Legend has it that Mary the Mother of Jesus appeared to Dominic at Prouille and urged him to preach the Rosary as a remedy against heresy. The Dominican devotion to the rosary, which enabled secular persons who did not understand Latin to follow or extend the rhythms of the choral office, is celebrated in Caravaggio's famous painting, "Madonna of the Rosary" (1607), and Dominican saints and blessed are subject matter for numerous works of art.

Very little is known directly about St. Dominic. His letter to the Nuns at Madrid in this book is a rare example of his writing. His interest in Dominican nuns has been maintained by Masters of the Order to this day, although at times the charge to provide for the care of the nuns has been contested. The 86th Master of the Order is Argentinian Father Carlos Azpiroz Costa, the second non-European Master of the Order. His nine-year term follows that of the first British Master of the Order, Timothy Radcliffe, whose address to the students of Yale University ends this volume. The Order's mission to proclaim the Gospel through whatever means possible and appropriate depends on the traditional Dominican life of study, community and preaching, and each aspect of Dominican life is further nourished by private or "secret" prayer. Dominic's "Nine Ways of Prayer" present the ways in which he was known to pray beyond his participation in liturgy and choral office.

The great hallmarks of preaching and study are conjoined in the life of Albert the Great (c. 1206–1280), whose "Commentary on Dionysius' Mystical Theology" demonstrates his, and the Order's, intellectual history. His "Treatise on the Manner of Praying" is example of the fact that Dominican intellectual life is always rooted in contemplation.

Perhaps the best known of Dominican intellectuals is Thomas Aquinas (c. 1225–1274) whose many works incorporate the secular knowledge of philosophy and present a reasoned understanding of the truths of Christian belief. His "Compendium of Theology" presents a catechism of sorts to be used by brother preachers, and treats faith, hope, and charity, the foundations of a graced life of prayer and service to others.

The earliest Dominican women are mostly unknown. They lived enclosed lives of prayer in cloistered convents under the care of the Friars. They and the many other women whose spiritual lives were guided toward the Dominican charism are represented by Mechtild of Magdeburg (1208–1282/1294). While Mechtild never actually became a Dominican, her book *The Flowering Light of the Godhead* bespeaks their secret lives of prayer. Mechtild also gives insight to the early troubles of the Order, and repeats Christ's promise to her that it will endure to the end of the world.

Meister Eckhart (c. 1260–1329), considered the father of German mysticism, is represented with his sermon on the Second Letter of Timothy. Here he considers the Dominican vocation to preaching in terms of the mystical life. His joyous acceptance of the mandate to "Speak the Word" conjoined with his understanding to "Work in all things" presents a spirituality totally dedicated to and flowing directly from the principals of Christian belief and of the Gospel that lead the individual to a Christlike perfection.

Catherine of Siena (1347–1380) lived the complete dedication Dominic prescribed and Eckhart elucidated. Her life of apostolic service as a Mantellata, essentially a secular third order Dominican, is centered on Truth. She is arguably the best known woman Dominican of history, and the section of her *Dialogue* on Truth gives mystical enlightenment to the intellectual quest.

Antonius Fierozzi (1389–1459), the prior who enabled the stunning Dominican artist Fra Angelico (c. 1400–1455), rejoices in the artistic work of God and of humans in the prologue of his *Summa Moralis*. The fine art of Fra Angelico is represented on the cover of this volume with the depiction of St. Dominic from "The Mocking of Christ" (1440–1441) his fresco measuring 188 x 164 cm or about two by three feet, which is in a cell on a upper floor of the Convento di San Marco, Florence. In Pius XII's words, reprinted in these pages, Fra Angelico's purpose was both to teach the truths of faith and to lead individuals to the practice of Christian virtues.

The Dominican charism of preaching spread to the New World with Bartolomé de Las Casas (1484–1566), whose preaching insisted that the rights and dignity of indigenous peoples be protected and respected. Las Cassas' instructions to preachers state the simple fact that preachers must live by their own words, for without the example of their own lives their preaching will remain unheard.

With the exception of some Mantellata, Dominican women remained mostly enclosed until modern times. Catherine de' Ricci (1522–1590) is remembered as mystic and stigmatic who identified wholly with the Passion of Christ in her writing and her life. Her letter to another enclosed nun in Italy gives advice and instruction on the vocation to prayer, especially within a community of Dominican women.

Martin de Porres (1579–1639) was a lay brother who lived in Peru during the height of Spain's colonial conquest of South America. The son of a Spanish nobleman and a freed black slave, he suffered the fate of an outsider, yet his simplicity allowed him to humbly hand forth the fruits of his contemplation. He is remembered in the canonization homily by Pope John XXIII as "Martin the Charitable."

Henri Dominique Lacordaire (1802–1861) was a young secular priest on his way to New York when the French revolution interrupted his plans in 1830. A brilliant orator, Lacordaire eventually determined his vocation was to help re-establish the Order of Preachers. He argues for its past and its future according to the founding vision of St. Dominic in an essay written shortly before he joined the Dominicans in 1839.

Rose Hawthorne Lathrop (1851–1926) also became a Dominican later in life, after the deaths of her husband and their child, through her vocation to nursing the dying poor. Her words from "Christ's Poor," an early magazine published by the "Hawthorne Dominicans" for friends and benefactors, show her complete dedication to apostolic ministry nourished by Dominican prayer and practice.

Georges-Yves Congar (1904–1995) devoted much of his prayer and study to ecumenism, particularly the relations with Protestant and Eastern Orthodox Churches, and his ecclesiology describes the pilgrim church enlivened by the Holy Spirit. The selections from his writings demonstrate the depth and breadth of his thinking after the Second Vatican Council.

Belgian- born Edward Schillebeeckx (1914–   ) is among Christianity's most prominent theologians. His writings explore every aspect of systematic theology, and are impossible to summarize. This book reproduces his classic essay on Dominican spirituality, in which he writes "a definitive all-round definition of Dominican spirituality cannot be given" because it has varied according to the local circumstances of culture, history, and church.

The book ends, then, with Timothy Radcliffe (1945–   ) 85th Master of the Order of Preachers, and his vision of the gospel to be preached within and without the walls of academe.

Each of the sixteen Dominicans whose lives and writings are presented in this volume has lived and preached the truth, the fruit of prayer, study, and Dominican community life. Their stories and their words follow.

The Dominican Tradition

The Dominican Tradition has its origin in the life and ministry of St. Dominic de Guzmán (1172–1221), the son of a Spanish noble, who founded one of the largest Orders in the Catholic Church. Dominic's charismatic vision of a way of responding to the needs of the church in the thirteenth century led to the establishment of the Order of Preachers, popularly known as the Dominicans.

The Thirteenth-Century World of Saint Dominic

The growth of an increasingly literate laity within the urban centers of thirteenth-century Italy and southern France posed a serious pastoral problem for the medieval church. These urbanized men and women experienced a strong dichotomy between the New Testament values of Christian life and the institutional church. The simplicity of Gospel living portrayed in the Acts of the Apostles, with its emphasis on shared common life and the preaching of the Good News of Jesus Christ in poverty, appealed to the hearts and minds of many and seemed to stand in stark contrast to the opulent lifestyle and moral laxity that often marked the clergy.

Because parish priests and the monks of the great abbeys seemed unable or unwilling to respond to their people's needs for forms of Christian life and spirituality more in accord with the apostolic life presented in the New Testament, the laity of the late twelfth and early thirteenth centuries in parts of France and Italy turned away from the institutional church in increasing numbers. Lay movements, such as the Poor Men of Lyons organized by Peter Valdes (d. 1218), who came to be called the Waldensians, offered an alternative form of Christian living that sought to imitate the simple life of the early church by an exact following of the gospel narratives on poverty and preaching.

At the same time the dualist doctrine of the third-century Persian religious thinker Mani (216–276) began to resurface in western Europe. Medieval followers of his dualism were called Manichees, Cathars, or Albigensians (from the town of Albi in southern France where dualism took hold). The Albigensians rejected most doctrines of the medieval church and taught that salvation was achieved by freeing oneself from everything material through a life of asceticism. The teachers of the movement, the Perfect, lived austere lives with special emphasis on fasting, chastity, poverty, and preaching.

The simultaneous emergence of the Waldensians and the Albigensians created the need for forms of Christian life and spirituality that provided patterns of Gospel living in accord with the traditional teachings of Christianity. Francis of Assisi (1182–1226) in Italy and Dominic de Guzmán (1170–1221) in Spain provided charismatic visions that would capture the ideals of the Gospel in new ways and draw many of the reform-minded men and women of the urban lay movements away from the Waldensians and the Albigensians and back into the medieval Catholic Church.

Saint Dominic, Canon Regular and Itinerant Preacher

Dominic de Guzmán completed his theological studies and was ordained a priest at Palencia in 1196. He became a Canon Regular (a member of a community of priests following the Rule of St. Augustine) of the cathedral of Osma in Spain. In 1203 Dominic encountered the Albigensians of southern France while on a diplomatic mission with his bishop, Diego de Acebes, to arrange a marriage between the son of King Alfonso VIII of Castile and the daughter of the King of Denmark. After the marriage negotiations failed in 1205, Dominic and Diego stopped at the papal court in Rome on their way back to Spain. Pope Innocent III (1198–1216) sent them to be part of the preaching mission against the Albigensians in Languedoc, the south of France. The nine years between 1206 and 1215 he spent preaching among the Albigensians taught Dominic a great deal about the impact of the Perfect on their followers. These years also served as the germinating period for the development of a charismatic vision of a way of living the Gospel in accord with the Christian faith that would appeal to the deepest ideals and needs of the men and women of his time.

Dominic's Vision of the Family of Contemplative Preachers

Dominic was guided by the image of the early Christian community in Jerusalem in the opening chapters of the Acts of the Apostles, which was at the heart of the spirituality he had known as a Canon Regular. He believed that the renewal of Christian society necessitated communities of men and women committed to living the apostolic life. The major component of that apostolic life was to be the preaching of the Gospel by members of communities that lived in evangelical poverty, who were devoted to contemplative prayer and engaged in constant study of the word of God. In Dominic's understanding, preachers were called to be the living reflection of the Gospel they proclaimed. Hence for him the vows of chastity, poverty, and obedience were meant to recreate and transform the preacher into an apostle, a living witness to the crucified and risen Lord, Jesus Christ.

During his early years of preaching in Languedoc, Dominic gathered a group of Albigensian women whom he had converted to form the nucleus of the first community of Dominican nuns. Through a life of contemplative prayer lived in a community dedicated to poverty and mutual service these Dominican women would incarnate the apostolic life and preach the Gospel by their witness to prayer and service. Although the Order of Preachers did not yet have official status, the first community of Dominican women at Prouille in the south of France, the preaching nuns, initiated an evolutionary development in which countless women in the centuries to come in collaboration with their Dominican brothers would fully participate in and help develop the life and ministry of the Order of Preachers, the Dominican family.

The Foundation of the Order of Friars Preachers

After the establishment of the Dominican nuns at Prouille, Dominic continued the implementation of his vision of communities of contemplative preachers living the apostolic life. In the spring of 1215, at the invitation of Bishop Fulk of Toulouse in southern France, Dominic brought the men who were his preaching companions in Languedoc to this important city to establish a formal religious community there under the direction of the bishop. Later in 1215, when Bishop Fulk set out to attend the Fourth Lateran Council in Rome, Dominic accompanied him, hoping to obtain papal approval for his new community of contemplative preachers. In accord with the legislation of the Council, Pope Innocent III promised Dominic that he would approve the founding of the new Order of Preachers after Dominic had chosen one of the already existing Rules of religious life.

As a Canon Regular of Osma, Dominic was already following the Rule of St. Augustine. He supplemented this rule with legislation and customs borrowed from the Premonstratensians, an order of Canons Regular founded by St. Norbert at Premontré in 1120, who supported his own vision of the apostolic life sustained by liturgical prayer. The spirituality of the Canons Regular was that of a community of religious priests who dedicated themselves to carrying out the daily liturgy of the church through the solemn celebration of Mass and the Divine Office and to caring for the sacramental needs of the faithful. Dominic joined these priestly ideals of the Canons Regular to a ministry of preaching in poverty (mendicancy) that flowed from a life of contemplation and study.

In December 1216, Pope Honorius III (1216–1227), the successor of Innocent III, approved Dominic's plan for an order of contemplative preachers exercising the priestly ministry and living in mendicant poverty. They owned no property except for the land on which their religious houses (priories) were built, and they were to work or beg for their daily needs. In the final four-and-a-half years of his life Dominic transformed the sixteen friars living in community at Toulouse into the international Order of Preachers whose lives and ministry would impact history until the present.

The Development of the Order of Preachers

In August 1217, Dominic sent seven friars to Paris to study, to teach, and to found a priory, and four to Spain to preach and establish priories. Three friars remained in Toulouse to continue the ministry they had begun under Bishop Fulk, and two friars went to Prouille to preach in Languedoc and to minister to the spiritual and temporal needs of the preaching nuns. Dominic himself set out for Rome to gain further support from Pope Honorius and to prepare the way for foundations in Italy. The years from 1217 to 1220 saw the growth of the Order through the reception of new members, the establishment of new priories, and the development of the preaching mission of the Order throughout Europe.

Under Dominic's direction, thirty representatives from the twelve priories in Europe gathered for General Chapters at Bologna in 1220 and 1221. The General Chapter of 1220 enacted legislation for preaching, formation of new members, studies, the observance of poverty, and the procedures for General Chapters. Dominic insisted that the Order's laws were not to bind under sin, and that the Priors had the power to dispense from the Order's laws when necessary for the sake of preaching or study.

The General Chapter of 1221 created Provinces as subdivisions of the Order; these would gather the priories of a certain geographic area under the authority of a Provincial, who was responsible to the Master of the Order. The twelve Provinces established by St. Dominic and the General Chapter were Spain, Provence, France, Lombardy, Tuscany, Germany, Hungary, England, Greece, Scandinavia, Poland, and the Holy Land. However, the most significant work of the Chapter, which ended six weeks before Dominic's death, was the formulation of the basic constitutional legislation that would concretize his vision and provide the flexibility for the subsequent development of the preaching mission of the Order.

The Dominican Family

The breadth and universality of Dominic's vision made it possible to incorporate a variety of men and women into the Dominican family. Traditionally the Order of Preachers has been divided into the First Order, the Second Order, and the Third Order.

The First Order, the Friars, is composed of clerical brothers and lay brothers. Clerical brothers are friars who are either priests engaged in ministry or students preparing for the priesthood. Cooperator brothers (formerly called lay brothers) are friars who once cared for the temporal needs of the community but who now also serve in a variety of other ministries, including the diaconate.

The Second Order is composed of contemplative nuns living in cloistered monasteries, usually under the jurisdiction of the local bishop. The Master of the Order also provides oversight and support for the nuns in their contemplative life.

The Third Order, which came into existence at the end of the thirteenth century, is divided into the Third Order Regular and the Third Order Secular. The Third Order Regular was initially composed of women who chose to live Dominican religious life without the strict rules of a cloistered monastery. In the nineteenth century the Third Order Regular also came to include Papal and Diocesan Congregations of Dominican Sisters established to engage in active ministries of service such as education and health care. Members of the Third Order Secular, originally called Tertiaries and now called the Dominican laity, are lay men and women living in the world. Their Rule states that "As members of the Order, they participate in its apostolic mission through prayer, study, and preaching according to the state of the laity."

Dominican Spirituality

The *Fundamental Constitution of the Order* (1968) reaffirms the preaching mission of the Order—"preaching and the salvation of souls"—and the means to attain this mission: (1) the three vows of obedience, chastity, and poverty; (2) community life with the monastic observances; (3) the solemn recitation of the Divine Office; and (4) the study of sacred truth.

The Vows of Obedience, Chastity, and Poverty

The purpose of the three vows within religious life is to free the individual to follow Jesus Christ. From the Dominican perspective the vows of obedience, chastity, and poverty free a man or woman to live the mystery of Jesus Christ the preacher. Dominican friars promise obedience to the Master of the Order, who is chosen by the brothers to hold the place of universal leadership once held by St. Dominic. The Order of Preachers views obedience as a relationship of mutual service between brothers committed to the common mission of preaching the Gospel. The Prior is the superior at the local level, the Provincial is the superior at the regional level, and the Master of the Order is the superior at the international level. Each serves as a focal point of unity and direction in the shared mission of preaching. Dominican obedience is the free choice of placing one's gifts at the disposal of the community, symbolized by the superior, for the sake of fulfilling the common preaching mission of the Order.

In the Dominican tradition the vow of chastity, like the vows of obedience and poverty, is related to the preaching mission of the Order. A Dominican man or woman chooses to live a celibate life within a community of contemplative preachers in order to share the family life of the Gospel community formed by the Holy Spirit through the proclamation and hearing of the word of God. A Dominican lives both in the family of other Dominican men and women committed to preaching and in the family of God's people, which he or she helps to create and sustain through the preaching of the Good News of Jesus Christ.

Since the lay movements of the thirteenth century saw evangelical poverty lived in apostolic simplicity as the guarantor of authentic preaching, the vow of poverty assumed special meaning within the Dominican tradition. Dominican friars were to be itinerant preachers living in mendicant poverty, to give up all possessions and fixed income, and to rely completely on the freewill offerings of the faithful. Each day the friars went out as mendicants begging for alms and their daily bread.

Community Life and the Monastic Observances

As the three vows of obedience, chastity, and poverty were understood as the first means of fulfilling the preaching mission of the Order, so community life with the monastic observances was seen to be the second means. The monastic observances within religious life, which Dominic received from the tradition of Benedictine monasticism, were silence, fasting, abstinence from meat, night vigils, the chapter of faults, acts of penance, and simplicity in religious attire and community life. Within the Dominican tradition the monastic observances provide a disciplined milieu in which contemplative preachers keep the word of God clearly focused in their minds and hearts as they prepare to engage in their ministry of preaching.

The Solemn Recitation of the Divine Office

The solemn recitation of the Divine Office, the Liturgy of the Hours, the third means of facilitating the preaching of the Gospel, centered the worship life of the community on the word of God. As a Canon Regular, Dominic had known the solemn celebration of the eight hours of the Divine Office: Matins, Lauds, Prime, Terce, Sext, None, Vespers, and Compline. With its patterns of hymns, psalms, Scripture readings, and prayers, the Office provided the place where a religious community daily encountered the word of God as it proclaimed the mysteries of salvation in the unfolding of the liturgical year. Daily Mass and the Divine Office constituted the common prayer of the community of contemplative preachers. Gathered together for prayer in common, they experienced the lifegiving water of the word of God and the living bread of the Holy Eucharist. This daily nourishment of word and sacrament strengthened and renewed the community of contemplative preachers so that they could share the same living water and bread of life with the people to whom they preached and ministered. The common praise of God and the hearing of the Good News were meant to be joyous occasions of new life and empowerment for ministry, which also would be strengthened by the fourth means of facilitating the preaching mission of the Order, the life of study.

The Study of Sacred Truth

The renewal of Christian life in the thirteenth century with its developing urban centers and its nascent universities not only required preachers who practiced poverty but also preachers who were learned in Scripture and the teachings of the church. For St. Dominic, study was essential to ensure the doctrinal preaching that was necessary to deal adequately with the intellectual challenge to the Catholic faith offered by the Waldensians and the Albigensians. The integral place of study in the Dominican tradition would give the preaching friars a profound role in the development of the great universities of medieval Europe. Every Dominican priory was a school for training contemplative preachers in Scripture and theology. The Dominican Order would provide the church with some of its greatest theologians and speculative thinkers, such as St. Albert the Great, St. Thomas Aquinas, Meister Eckhart, and St. Antoninus.

The vows of obedience, chastity, and poverty; community life with the monastic observances; the celebration of the Divine Office; and continuous study of Scripture and the truths of faith were meant to provide the contemplative basis for Dominican preaching. The fulfillment of St. Dominic's vision of a community of contemplative preachers requires a careful balancing so that both the active-preaching dimension and the contemplative-prayer-study dimension are held in creative tension.

This common framework for understanding the Dominican tradition in terms of the end and the four means was in use from the thirteenth century until 1968. The General Chapter of 1968 kept the traditional understanding for the First Order, but left the Second and Third Orders free to adapt the traditional understanding to their own Dominican experience in their own Constitutions. Hence while the Fundamental Constitution of the Order presents the guiding vision for the whole Dominican family, the Second Order (nuns) and the Third Order Regular (sisters) and Third Order Secular (laity) each have their own Constitutions that articulate their appropriation of the Fundamental Constitution. Thus congregations of Dominican sisters and the

Dominican laity in the United States present the Four Elements or Four Pillars in many revised Constitutions in the 1970s: community, prayer, study, and ministry. In these perspectives the vows are subsumed under the larger umbrella of community. The discussion of community includes the vows, prayer and study follow next, and everything is drawn together in ministry.

Independent of the various emphases placed on the guiding vision of St. Dominic, all Dominican men and women commit themselves through vows or promises to live in communities where common prayer and study enable them to preach the Gospel through diverse forms of ministry.

Thomas C. McGonigle, o.p.

Saint Dominic (1171–1221)

D ominic de Guzmán was born in Caleruega, Spain, about twenty miles from the Cathedral of El Burgo de Osma, in 1170 or 1171. His parents, Felix de Guzmán and Jane de Aza, were of minor nobility, she of higher rank than he. They were a pious family: one of Dominic's uncles was a priest, and eventually not only Dominic but his two brothers (Anthony and Mannes) as well as two sons of his sister, would become priests. All but Anthony, a Canon of Saint James, became Dominicans.

Despite his evident fame there is relatively little biographical material available about Dominic. The earliest and most authentic source document is the *Libellus* of Blessed Jordan of Saxony, the Second Master General of the Order, written sometime between December 1231 and July 1234. Even though the *Libellus* is ten years removed from the death of Dominic, Jordan had access to his own and others' direct memories of Dominic. Hence at least three friars said to have belonged to the first group of Dominic's followers—Peter Seila, Bertrand of Garrigua, and John of Navarre—and others were able to provide testimony to Jordan as he wrote the story of the beginnings of the Order.

There are many other early writings, including those of Peter of Ferrand, Constantine of Orvieto, Blessed Humbert of Romans (fifth Master General), Bartholomew of Trent, Stephen of Bourbon, Thomas of Cantimpré, Gerard of Frachet, Stephen of Salagnac, and Dietrich of Apolda, that seek to trace the life and works of the Canon of Osma who began a preaching of the Gospel that has encircled the world.

There is a legend, possibly true, that Dominic early preferred penance to comfort; it is said that as a child he preferred the hard floor to his soft bed. His Gospel charity is also well attested. Dominic entered studies at Palencia in the kingdom of Leon when he was 14, and while there sold his few possessions to aid those suffering from a famine. In 1190, at

1

the age of about twenty, Dominic became a member of the canonry at Osma, and was ordained to priesthood about five years later. The canonry, a communal foundation for secular clerics, followed the Rule of St. Augustine. Dominic, who was sub-prior by the time he was about thirty, was especially fond of studying the *Conferences* of John Cassian.

Dominic's travels with his bishop and his preaching against the heretical Albigensians are well known, and as he gathered followers the concept of a religious order dedicated to preaching must have formed in his mind and heart. But the first "Dominicans" were women. Reportedly, late on July 22, 1206 (the feast of Saint Mary Magdalene), Dominic saw a sphere of fire descending on a shrine to Mary on a hill overlooking the village of Prouille. Dominic took this to be a sign of God (a *Seignadou*) as it continued for two additional nights, which called him to found a monastery of nuns at Prouille. He soon converted nine women and opened the first "Dominican" convent five short months later, on December 27, 1206, under the patronage of Saint Mary Magdalene.

He ate and slept little, wore a hair shirt, and walked unshod between towns, attracting followers and converts along the way. He preferred living charity and humility to creating a wordstorm of fire and brimstone, characteristic traits of the Order of Preachers soon to come from his leadership and his holiness. His canonization process attested to the efficacy of his prayer. It is reported that in 1211, in the midst of fierce warfare between the Albigensians and papal forces, a boat carrying a group of English pilgrims overturned in the Garonne River. Dominic prostrated himself in prayer and demanded their safety in the name of Jesus Christ, which favor was granted. Lawrence, a rescued pilgrim, would be among Dominic's first followers.

He attracted other followers in Toulouse and Castres, and in 1215 Dominic made his way to the Lateran Council in Rome, where he may have encountered St. Francis of Assisi. Both Orders call their founders "Holy Father," and each has looked to the other for an example of simplicity. For hundreds of years Dominicans and Franciscans have shared the celebration of each other's founder: Dominicans invite a Franciscan to preach on the Feast of St. Dominic (August 8), while Franciscans invite a Dominican to preach on the Feast of St. Francis (October 4). Each Order was approved by Pope Innocent III, clearly with the belief that they would help hold the church together as the raucous thirteenth century lurched forward. Innocent III's foresight joined Dominic's vision. Heretofore only bishops had preached, or approved preaching, within their own dioceses. But Dominic's wandering band of apostolic preachers could cross diocesan boundaries. Dominic wrote *Constitutions* to delimit the *Rule of St. Augustine,* which he chose for his Order. Friars would not be bound by stability to one house, and the monastic horarium would be adapted to suit their apostolic mission. By the summer of 1216 their number had grown to sixteen, and Bishop Folques of Toulouse, whom Dominic had accompanied to the Lateran Council, gave the Order charge of three churches.

When Pope Honorius III succeeded Innocent III in August 1216, Dominic traveled to Rome to obtain the papal bull confirming the establishment of the Order. He waited three months and received it December 22, 1216. The same day Honorius issued a second bull making the Order of Friars Preachers a papal order:

> We, considering that the brethren of the Order will be the champions of the faith and true lights of the world, do confirm the Order in all its lands and possessions present and to come, and we take under our protection and government the Order itself, with all its goods and rights.

Pope Honorious III also appointed Dominic Master of the Sacred Palace—theological advisor to the Pope—a position thenceforth ordinarily held by a Dominican. Dominic returned to Toulouse in May 1217 and planned to send the Friars on preaching mission on the feast of the Assumption, August 15. He met their opposition simply and with prescience: the seed would molder if hoarded, he said, but it would grow and multiply if scattered. They went to Rome and to Spain, they preached in the south of France; with Dominic as first Master of the Order they undertook study—first in Paris and Bologna—as a critical part of their formation, and professors were among those to enter the Order.

The Order grew in numbers and in influence as friars and friaries multiplied and the success of Dominic's reforms spread. Pope Honorious III asked Dominic to reform the various independent convents of nuns in Rome, which task he substantially began by February, 1220. He closed convents, moving many of the nuns to San Sisto, a monastery given him by the Pope for his friars, and called a nun from Prouille to oversee the new community of nuns. Dominic moved with the friars to the men's convent adjacent to the Church of Santa Sabina all'Aventino, which had been given over to them by the Pope in 1218, and which was repurchased (from the Italian government) in 1929 to house the headquarters of the Masters of the Order to this day. Over time Santa Sabina was the monastic home of Dominican saints Hyacinth (1185–1257), Thomas Aquinas (c. 1225–1274), and Pope Pius V (1504–1572), among others.

Dominic called the first General Chapter of the Order at Bologna near Pentecost 1220. There his concept of fiduciary control by the lay brothers was outvoted. No matter the topic, the fact that the founder and Master of the Order could be outvoted struck a high note in the development of democratic governance of religious orders. During the intervening year between the first and second General Chapters, Dominic preached throughout Italy. After the second General Chapter, also at Bologna, Dominic's health began to fail. He died on the Feast of the Transfiguration, August 6, 1221. He was fifty-one years old.

Dominic's vision did not end with his death, and reports of miracles attributed to his intercession led to such great numbers of pilgrims to his tomb that in May 1233 his body was transferred to a larger space. Within a year he was canonized.

Dominic was a preacher, not a writer, and there are only three examples of his writings left to history. Each bespeaks his own penances, and the letter to the Prioress and the Entire Community of Nuns at Madrid that follows characteristically urges penance and strict observance of the rule and constitutions. His spirituality is solidly planted in a foundation of prayer, community, study, and preaching, and his nine ways of prayer present an old-yet-new means of worship.

Phyllis Zagano

From *The Letters of St. Dominic*

Friar Dominic, Master of the Preachers, to the Beloved Prioress and the Entire Community of Nuns at Madrid: Health and Daily Progress,

Greatly do we rejoice and thank God because of your holy life and because He has freed you from the corruption of this world. Daughters, fight the ancient adversary insistently with fasting, for only he will be crowned who has striven according to the rules. If until the present you have not had a place in which to live your religious life, now you can no longer be excused, because by the grace of God you have buildings suitable enough for living the religious life. From now on I want silence to be kept in the forbidden places, the refectory, the dormitory, and the oratory, and your law to be observed in all other matters. Let none go out through the gate and no one enter except the bishop or some prelate for the sake of preaching or making a visitation. Be not sparing of discipline and vigils. Be obedient to your prioress. Avoid talking idly to one another. Let not your time be wasted in conversation.

Since we cannot help you in temporalities, we do not want to give any friar the authority to receive postulants, but only the prioress with the council of her community. Moreover, we command our dear brother, i.e., Friar Mannes, who has worked so hard and has joined you to this blessed state, that he arrange and dispose everything as shall seem good to him, so you might live a most religious and most holy life. Furthermore, we give him power to visit and correct and to remove the prioress (if it be necessary) with the consent of the majority of the nuns; and we give him permission that he may grant dispensations in some matters, if it seems fit to him.

Farewell in Christ.

* * *

The Nine Ways of Prayer of St. Dominic

Holy teachers like Augustine, Ambrose, Gregory, Hilary, Isidore, John Chrysostom, John Damascene, Bernard, and other saintly Greek and Latin doctors have discoursed on prayer at great length. They have encouraged and described it, pointed out its necessity and value, explained the method, the dispositions which are required, and the impediments which stand in its way. In learned books, the glorious and venerable doctor, Brother Thomas Aquinas, and Albert, of the Order of Preachers, as well as William in his treatise on the virtues, have considered admirably and in a holy, devout, and beautiful manner that form of prayer in which the soul makes use of the members of the body to raise itself more devoutly to God. In this way the soul, in moving the body, is moved by it. At times it becomes rapt in ecstasy as was Saint Paul, or is caught up in a rapture of the spirit like the prophet David. Saint Dominic often prayed in this way, and it is fitting that we say something of his method.

Certainly many saints of both the Old and New Testament are known to have prayed like this at times. Such a method serves to enkindle devotion by the alternate action of soul upon body and body upon soul. Prayer of this kind would cause Saint Dominic to be bathed in tears, and would arouse the fervor of his holy will to such intensity that his bodily members could not be restrained from manifesting his devotion by certain signs. As a result, the spirit of the supplicant was sometimes raised up during its entreaties, petitions, and thanksgivings.

The following, then, are the special modes of prayer, besides those very devout and customary forms, which Saint Dominic used during the celebration of Mass and the praying of the psalmody. In choir or along the road, he was often seen lifted suddenly out of himself and raised up with God and the angels.

The First Way of Prayer

Saint Dominic's first way of prayer was to humble himself before the altar as if Christ, signified by the altar, were truly and personally present and not in symbol alone. He would say with Judith: "O Lord God, the prayer of the humble and the meek hath always pleased Thee [*Judith* 9:16]." *It was through humility that the Chanaanite woman and the prodigal son obtained what they desired; as for me,* "I am not worthy that Thou shouldst come under my roof" [*Matt* 8:8] *for* "I have been humbled before you exceedingly, O Lord [*Ps* 118:107]."

In this way our holy father, standing erect, bowed his head and humbly considering Christ, his Head, compared his lowliness with the excellence of Christ. He then gave himself completely in showing his veneration. The brethren were taught to do this whenever they passed before the humiliation of the Crucified One in order that Christ, so greatly humbled for us, might see us humbled before his majesty. And he commanded the friars to humble themselves in this way before the entire Trinity whenever they chanted solemnly: "Glory be to the Father, and to the Son, and to the Holy Spirit." In this manner of profoundly inclining his head, as shown in the drawing, Saint Dominic began his prayer.

The Second Way of Prayer

Saint Dominic used to pray by throwing himself outstretched upon the ground, lying on his face. He would feel great remorse in his heart and call to mind those words of the Gospel, saying sometimes in a voice loud enough to be heard: "O God, be merciful to me, a sinner" [*Luke* 18:13]. With devotion and reverence he repeated that verse of David: "I am he that has sinned, I have done wickedly" [*II Kings* 24:17]. Then he would weep and groan vehemently and say: "I am not worthy to see the heights of heaven because of the greatness of my iniquity, for I have aroused thy anger and done what is evil in thy sight." From the psalm: "Deus auribus nostris audivimus" he said fervently and devoutly: "For our soul is cast down to the dust, our belly is flat on the earth!" [*Ps* 43:25]. To this he would add: "My soul is prostrate in the dust; quicken thou me according to thy word" [*Ps* 118:25].

Wishing to teach the brethren to pray reverently, he would sometimes say to them: *When those devout Magi entered the dwelling they found the child with Mary, his mother, and falling down they worshipped him. There is no doubt that we too have found the God-Man with Mary, his handmaid.* "Come, let us adore and fall down in prostration before God, and let us weep before God, and let us weep before the Lord that made us" [*Ps* 94:6]. He would also exhort the young men, and say to them: *If you cannot weep for your own sins because you have none, remember that there are many sinners who can be disposed for mercy and charity. It was for these that the prophets lamented; and when Jesus saw them, he wept bitterly.* The holy David also wept as he said: "I beheld the transgressors and began to grieve" [*Ps* 118:158].

The Third Way of Prayer

At the end of the prayer which has just been described, Saint Dominic would rise from the ground and give himself the discipline with an iron chain, saying, "Thy discipline has corrected me unto the end" [*Ps* 17:36]. This is why the Order decreed, in memory of his example, that all the brethren should receive the discipline with wooden switches upon their shoulders as they were bowing down in worship and reciting and psalm "Miserere" or "De Profundis" after Compline on ferial days. This is performed for their own faults or for those of others whose alms they receive and rely upon. No matter how sinless he may be, no one is to desist from this holy example.

The Fourth Way of Prayer

After this Saint Dominic would remain before the altar or in the chapter room with his gaze fixed on the Crucified One, looking upon Him with perfect attention. He genuflected frequently, again and again. He would continue sometimes from after Compline until midnight, now rising, now kneeling again, like the apostle Saint James, or the leper of the gospel who said on bended knee: "Lord, if thou wilt, thou canst make me clean" [*Matt* 8:2]. He was like Saint Stephen who knelt and called out with a loud cry: "Lord, do not lay this sin against them" [*Acts* 7:60]. Thus there was formed in our holy father, Saint Dominic, a great confidence in God's mercy towards himself, all sinners, and for the perseverance of the younger brethren whom he sent forth to preach to souls. Sometimes he could not even restrain his voice, and the friars would hear him murmuring: "Unto thee will I cry, O Lord: O my God, be not thou silent to me: lest if thou be silent to me, I become like them that go down into the pit" [*Ps* 27:1] and comparable phrases from the Sacred Scripture.

At other times, however, he spoke within himself and his voice could not be heard. He would remain in genuflection for a long while, rapt in spirit; on occasion, while in this position, it appeared from his face that his mind had penetrated heaven and soon he reflected an intense joy as he wiped away the flowing tears. He was in a stage of longing and anticipation like a thirsty man who has reached a spring, and like a traveler who is at last approaching his homeland. Then he would become more absorbed and ardent as moved in an agile manner but with great grace, now arising, now genuflecting. He was so accustomed to bend his knees to God in this way that when he traveled, in the inns after a weary journey, or along the wayside while his companions rested or slept, he would return to these genuflections, his own intimate and personal form of worship. This way of prayer he taught his brethren more by example than by words.

The Fifth Way of Prayer

When he was in the convent, our holy father Dominic would sometimes remain before the altar, standing erect without supporting himself or leaning upon anything. Often his hands would be extended before his breast in the manner of an open book; he would stand with great reverence and devotion as if reading in the very presence of God. Deep in prayer, he appeared to be meditating upon the words of God, and he seemed to repeat them to himself in a sweet voice. He regularly prayed in this way for it was Our Lord's manner as Saint Luke tells us: ". . . according to his custom he entered the synagogue on the Sabbath and began to read" [*Luke* 4:16]. The psalmist also tells us that "Phinees stood up and prayed, and the slaughter ceased" [*Ps* 105:30].

He would sometimes join his hands, clasping them firmly together before eyes filled with tears and restrain himself. At other times he would raise his hands to his shoulders as the priest does at Mass. He appeared then to be listening carefully as if to hear something spoken from the altar. If one had seen his great devotion as he stood erect and prayed, he would certainly have thought that he was observing a prophet, first speaking with an angel or with God himself, then listening, then silently thinking of those things which had been revealed to him.

On a journey he would secretly steal away at the time for prayer and, standing, would immediately raise his mind to heaven. One would then have heard him speaking sweetly and with supreme delight some loving words from his heart and from the riches of Holy Scripture which he seemed to draw from the fountains of the Savior. The friars were very much moved by the sight of their father and master praying in this manner. Thus, having become more fervent, they were instructed in the way of reverent and constant prayer: "Behold as the eyes of servants are on the hands of their masters, as the eyes of the handmaid are on the hands of her mistress . . ." [*Ps* 122:2].

The Sixth Way of Prayer

Our Holy Father, Saint Dominic, was also seen to pray standing erect with his hands and arms outstretched forcefully in the form of a cross. He prayed in this way when God, through his supplications, raised to life the boy Napoleon in the sacristy of the Church of Saint Sixtus in Rome, and when he was raised from the ground at the celebration of Mass, as the good and holy Sister Cecilia, who was present with many other people and saw him, narrates. He was like Elias who stretched himself out and lay upon the widow's son when he raised him to life.

In a similar manner he prayed near Toulouse when he delivered the group of English pilgrims from danger of drowning in the river. Our Lord prayed thus while hanging on the cross, that is, with his hands and arms extended and "with a loud cry and tears . . . he was heard because of his reverent submission" [*Heb* 5:7].

Nor did the holy man Dominic resort to this manner of praying unless he was inspired by God to know that something great and marvelous was to come about through the power of his prayer. Although he did not forbid the brethren to pray in this way, neither did he encourage them to do so. We do not know what he said when he stood with his hands and arms extended in the form of a cross and raised the boy to life. Perhaps it was those words of Elias: "O Lord, my God, let the soul of this child, I beseech thee, return into his body" (III Kings 17:21). He certainly followed the prophet's exterior manner in his prayers on that occasion. The friars and sisters, however, as well as the nobles and cardinals, and all others present were so struck by this most unusual and astonishing way of prayer that they failed to remember the words he spoke. Afterwards, they did not feel free to ask Dominic about these matters because this holy and remarkable man inspired in them a great sense of awe and reverence by reason of the miracle.

In a grave and mature manner, he would slowly pronounce the words in the Psalter which mention this way of prayer. He used to say attentively: "O Lord, the God of my salvation: I have cried in the day and in the night before thee," as far as that verse "All the day I have cried to thee, O Lord: I stretched out my hands to thee" (*Ps* 87:2-10). Then he would add: "Hear, O Lord, my prayer, give ear to my supplication in thy truth . . ." He would continue the prayer to these words: "I stretched forth my hands to thee . . . Hear me speedily, O Lord" [*Ps* 142:1-7].

This example of our father's prayer would help devout souls to appreciate more easily his great zeal and wisdom in praying thus. This is true whether, in doing so, he wished to move God in some wonderful manner through his prayer or whether he felt through some interior inspiration that God was to move him to seek some singular grace for himself or his neighbor. He then shone with the spiritual insight of David, the ardor of Elias, the charity of Christ, and with a profound devotion.

The Seventh Way of Prayer

While praying he was often seen to reach towards heaven like an arrow which has been shot from a taut bow straight upwards into the sky. He would stand with hands outstretched above his head and joined together, or at times slightly separated as if about to receive something from heaven. One would believe that he was receiving an increase of grace and in this rapture of spirit was asking God for the gifts of the Holy Spirit for the Order he had founded.

He seemed to seek for himself and his brethren something of that transcendent joy which is found in living the beatitudes, praying that each would consider himself truly blessed in extreme poverty, in bitter mourning, in cruel persecutions, in a great hunger and thirst for justice, in anxious mercy towards all. His entreaty was that his children would find their delight in observing the commandments and in the perfect practice of the evangelical counsels. Enraptured, the holy father then appeared to have entered into the Holy of Holies and the Third Heaven. After prayer of this kind he truly seemed to be a prophet, whether in correcting the faulty, in directing others, or in his preaching.

Our holy father did not remain at prayer of this type very long but gradually regained full possession of his faculties. He looked during that time like a person coming from a great distance or like a stranger in this world, as could easily be discerned from his countenance and manner. The brethren would then hear him praying aloud and saying as the prophet: "Hear, O Lord, the voice of my supplication which I pray to thee, when I lift up my hands to thy holy temple" [*Ps* 27:2].

Through his words and holy example he constantly taught the friars to pray in this way, often repeating those phrases from the psalms: "Behold, now bless ye the Lord, all ye servants of the Lord . . . in the nights lift up your hands to the holy places, and bless ye the Lord" (*Ps* 133:13), "I have cried to thee, O Lord, hear me; hearken to my voice when I cry to thee. Let my prayer be directed as incense in thy sight; the lifting up of my hands as the evening sacrifice" (*Ps* 140:1-2). The drawing shows us this mode of prayer so that we may better understand it.

The Eighth Way of Prayer

Our father, Saint Dominic, had yet another manner of praying at once beautiful, devout, and pleasing, which he practiced after the canonical hours and the thanksgiving following meals. He was then zealous and filled with the spirit of devotion which he drew from the divine words which had been sung in the choir or refectory. Our father quickly withdrew to some solitary place, to his cell or elsewhere, and recollected himself in the presence of God. He would sit quietly, and after the sign of the cross, begin to read from a book opened before him. His spirit would then be sweetly aroused as if he heard Our Lord speaking, as we are told in the psalms: "I will hear what the Lord God will speak to me . . . (*Ps* 84:9). As if disputing with a companion he would first appear somewhat impatient in his thought and words. At the next moment he would become a quiet listener, then again seem to discuss and contend. He seemed almost to laugh and weep at the same time, and then, attentively and submissively, would murmur to himself and strike his breast.

Should some curious person have desired to watch our holy father Dominic, he would have appeared to him like Moses who went into the desert, to Horeb, the sacred mountain of God, and there beheld the burning bush and heard the Lord speaking to him as he was bowed down in the divine presence. This holy custom of our father seems, as it were, to resemble the prophetic mountain of the Lord inasmuch as he quickly passed upwards from reading to prayer, from prayer to meditation, and from meditation to contemplation.

When he read alone in this solitary fashion, Dominic used to venerate the book, bow to it, and kiss it. This was especially true if he was reading the Gospels and when he had been reading the very words which had come from the mouth of Christ. At other times he would hide his face and cover it with his cappa, or bury his face in his hands and veil it slightly with the capuce. Then he would weep, all fervent and filled with holy desires. Following this, as if to render thanks to some person of great excellence for benefits received, he would reverently rise and incline his head for a short time. Wholly refreshed and in great interior peace, he then returned to his book.

The Ninth Way of Prayer

Our father, Saint Dominic, observed this mode of prayer while traveling from one country to another, especially when he passed through some deserted region. He then delighted in giving himself completely to meditation, disposing for contemplation, and he would say to his companion on the journey: *It is written in Osee* "I will lead her (my spouse) into the wilderness and I will speak to her ear" (*Osee* 2:14). Parting from his companion, he would go on ahead or, more frequently, follow at some distance. Thus withdrawn, he would walk and pray; in his meditation he was inflamed and the fire of charity was enkindled. While he prayed it appeared as if he were brushing dust or bothersome flies from his face when he repeatedly fortified himself with the Sign of the Cross.

The brethren thought that it was while praying in this way that the saint obtained his extensive penetration of Sacred Scripture and profound understanding of the divine words, the power to preach so fervently and courageously, and that intimate acquaintance with the Holy Spirit by which he came to know the hidden things of God.

Albert the Great (c. 1206–1280)

Albert the Great was born of a knightly family near Ulm, Germany in 1206. He went to study at the University of Padua around 1221 and became very interested in natural science and theology. Here he was introduced to the works of Aristotle and first met the Dominicans.

Jordan of Saxony, Dominic's successor as Master of the Order of Friars Preachers, came to Padua in 1223 seeking recruits among the students of the university. Albert was among the students who responded to his invitation. Since there was no Dominican priory at that time in Padua, Albert was sent back to Germany to do his novitiate and begin his theological studies. In 1233 he was appointed lector in theology successively at the Dominican priories in Hildesheim, Freiburg im Breisgau, Regensburg, Strasbourg, and Cologne. After this important teaching internship Albert was sent to the University of Paris in the early 1240s to do his doctorate in theology.

In the first dispersal of the friars in 1217, Dominic sent seven of the sixteen members of the Order to Paris to study and become learned in the sacred sciences so that they would be adequately prepared to exercise their ministry of preaching and eventually teaching. When he visited Paris in 1219 Dominic found a community of thirty friars, many of them recruited from the students at the University of Paris, which had received papal approval from Innocent III in 1215. Soon young Dominicans were being sent from newly established priories all over Europe to study at Paris in order to serve as lectors of theology within the Order.

Roland of Cremona was already a Master of Arts at Bologna when he entered the Order in 1219. After he had served as lector of theology in several Dominican priories, Jordan of Saxony sent him to Paris in 1228 to study under John of St. Giles. Because of his previous studies and his teaching experience, Roland became the first Dominican to become a doctor of theology at the University of Paris in 1229; he would hold one of the twelve chairs in theology at the university. The Dominicans would gain a second chair in theology when John of St. Giles himself chose to enter the Order.

When Albert came to Paris in the early 1240s he studied under Gueric of Saint-Quentin, the successor of John of St. Giles. In the midst of his doctoral studies Albert became more and more convinced of the importance of the thought of Aristotle for his work, as the full Aristotelian corpus was being received in the Latin-speaking West along with the commentaries of Jewish and Muslim scholars. Albert became a doctor of theology in 1245 at the University of Paris, where he held one of the two Dominican chairs in theology from 1245 to 1248.

Thomas Aquinas, as a young Dominican, was sent to study under Albert in 1246. The notes Thomas took during Albert's lectures on the *Nicomachean Ethics* of Aristotle have been preserved. It was the beginning of a lifetime of fraternal and scholarly collaboration between the two great Dominican doctors of the church.

In 1248 Albert and Thomas went to Cologne, where Albert supervised the foundation of a new general house of studies for the Dominican Order. While he was teaching at Cologne, Albert lectured on the writings of Pseudo-Dionysius and Aristotle's ethics. Albert's commitment both to the Neoplatonic thought, represented by Pseudo-Dionysius, and to making Aristotle intelligible to the Latin West was profoundly significant for the development of the Dominican intellectual tradition. Although he did not hesitate to correct Aristotle's views when he thought they were wrong, Albert also believed that the use of Aristotle could be profoundly helpful in developing the positive Christian vision that understands human life as grace perfecting nature.

From 1254 to 1257 Albert served the preaching mission of the Order as Provincial of Germany. He oversaw Dominican friars in thirty-six priories and perhaps as many monasteries of Dominican nuns in Germany, Austria, Switzerland, Belgium, and the Netherlands.

After his service as Provincial, Albert returned to his teaching in Cologne until he was appointed Bishop of Regensburg in 1260 by Pope Alexander IV. He was an excellent pastor and administrator and brought order and renewed spiritual life to what had been a troubled diocese. Pope Urban IV accepted his resignation as bishop in 1263, and he returned to Germany where he resumed his preaching and teaching at Würzburg, Strasbourg, and finally from 1270 to 1277 back at Cologne.

Albert came to the defense of the teachings of Thomas Aquinas in 1277, three years after his former student's death. After a life dedicated to preaching and teaching in which he sought to witness to the complementarity of faith and reason in the proclamation of the Gospel, Albert died at Cologne in 1280. He was canonized and declared a doctor of the church by Pope Pius XI in 1931. Pope Pius XII named him the patron of natural scientists in 1941. The selections that follow are from Albert's *Commentary on Dionysius' Mystical Theology* and *A Treatise on the Manner of Praying.*

Thomas C. McGonigle, o.p.

From *Commentary on Dionysius' Mystical Theology*

(1) Moses appears to have seen God himself. It is God himself who is seen in face-to-face vision, because this is what is promised us in heaven by the apostle (1 Cor 13:12). But this is how Moses saw God, because it says of him in Exodus 33:11, "The Lord spoke to Moses face to face." Otherwise his prayer would have been in vain, "Show me your face" (Exod 33:13). So he appears to have seen God himself.

(2) How is it possible that one could be contemplating God in the noblest kind of contemplation and yet not see God himself, as Moses did? And since many things come together in our natural intellectual processes—the abstraction of forms from images, their union with the possible intellect and the illumination by the agent intellect—to which of these is the knowledge involved in such exalted contemplation to be assimilated?

In response we must say that Moses did not see God himself in himself, he saw him in his most noble effects, effects of grace and of theophanies, the latter being manifested images of the divine goodness.

So we may answer the points raised as follows:

(1) "Seeing the face" can mean two different things. If it is taken to mean seeing God's face in itself, without any veil, then this is how it will be seen in heaven, but it is not how Moses saw it; Moses saw God's face in certain signs of God's effects, which Dionysius here calls "subordinate principles," and in the passage of scripture referred to they are called God's "back" (Exod 33:23). So the Lord said to him, "You will see my back, but my face you will not be able to see."

(2) There is a link-up of lights in sense-perception, and there is a similar link-up of intellectual lights. Now the things of God cannot be learned from any kind of probable or necessary inferences from first principles, and the light of the agent intellect has no other tools which it can wield as its own except first principles; so if it is to know the things of God it needs the light of the angels' intellect to come to it, which effects a variety of appearances in our souls in which the things of God are seen, reflecting the more unified way in which these appearances exist in the angels themselves, as was explained in the *Celestial Hierarchy*. The philosopher too says in his *Divination in Dreams* that because they cannot be arrived at by way of any systematic speculation on the basis of first principles; the intellect receives them by being united to some higher moving powers. It is much more the case that the soul is fortified to see the things of God by having the divine light coming down into it. Maybe both procedures are combined. And this light is called the "mirror of eternity," in which the prophets saw their visions. But it is not God, it merely comes from God, and it is the equivalent of the light of the agent intellect in the case of natural knowledge. These are the "declarations" of which Dionysius speaks here, which he also calls "divine objects of sight." This makes it clear how it is not God himself who is seen even in the most noble forms of contemplation, and this answers our question.

From *A Treatise on the Manner of Praying*

"On preparation for prayer."

We should prepare ourselves for prayer. This preparation is of two kinds: remote and immediate.

Similarly remote preparation is of two kinds: interior and exterior. Interior preparation consists in three things. First, there is the purification of the conscience: *If our hearts do not reprove us, we have this confidence in God: that God hears us whenever we ask for anything.* Secondly, there is the humbling of the mind, for *the Lord hears the cry of the humble and does not spurn their petition.* Thirdly, there is the forgiveness of injuries: *Whenever you stand to pray, forgive, if you have anything against anyone; so that your Father in heaven may in turn forgive you your trespasses.*

Exterior preparation likewise consists in three things. First, there is the fulfillment of the commandments of God, for as Saint

Isidore said: "If we do what the Lord commands, we will without doubt obtain what we ask for." Secondly, there is reconciliation with anyone we have offended: *If you bring your gift to the altar and there recall that your brother or sister has anything against you, leave your gift before the altar and go; first be reconciled with your brother or sister and then come and offer your gift.* Thirdly, there is the practice of fasting and almsgiving which supports prayer, for Isaiah says: *Share your bread with the hungry and take the poor and homeless into your house; then when you call, the Lord will hear you.*

Immediate preparation is likewise of two kinds: again, interior and exterior. Interior preparation consists in three things. First, there is personal recollection: *Whenever you pray, go into your room, close the door, and pray to your Father in private.* Entering into your room is that personal recollection of the heart and closing the door is the maintenance of a spirit of recollection. Personal recollection is accomplished by gathering within oneself the thoughts and emotions which have had free range.

Secondly, we focus our attention upon the Lord. For we pray in truth when we do not think about other matters. Thus, the soul must first be purified and thoughts about temporal concerns must be set aside so that the pure eye of the heart may be directed truely and simply to the Lord. Let every carnal or worldly thought depart, lest the soul think of anything else than that alone for which it prays. The priest in proclaiming the preface prepares our hearts by saying: "Lift up your hearts," to which we reply: "We lift them up to the Lord." Thus, the heart is closed to its adversary and opened to God alone, lest we have one thing in our hearts and another on our lips.

How can you be heard by God, you ask, when you cannot hear yourself? You want the Lord to be mindful of you when you are not mindful of yourself! This is to offend the majesty of God by negligence in prayer. This is to watch with the eyes and sleep with the heart, while the Christian ought to be watching with the heart even while sleeping. Thirdly, there is the stirring up of devotion to God, which is brought about especially by meditating upon our miserable condition and upon the goodness and mercy of God. In meditating upon our miserable condition we learn what it is necessary to ask for, and in meditating upon the mercy of God we learn with what devotion we ought to ask.

[Exterior preparation consists in three things, namely, place, appearance and gesture. With regard to place it is certain that one can pray while standing as well as sitting, or even while lying down. Nevertheless in public prayer we ought to observe the form established by the Church or by the majority of us. With regard to appearance keep in mind that a humble and abject demeanor is appropriate to prayer. With regard to gesture note that it includes genuflecting, lifting up one's hands, striking the breast, raising or lowering the eyes and countenance, closing the lips or silencing the voice, the shedding of tears, the emitting of groans, sighing, etc.]

Thomas Aquinas (c. 1225–1274)

Thomas Aquinas was born at Roccasecca near Naples in 1225 or 1226, the youngest son of a large family of the lower nobility. He spent his early years from 1230 until 1239 at the famous Benedictine Abbey of Monte Cassino. His family sent him to study the liberal arts at the University of Naples when he was fourteen, and it was here that he was attracted to the newly founded Order of Friars Preachers in 1243. Although Thomas' family initially opposed his Dominican vocation, they eventually allowed him to enter the Order. He was sent to St. Jacques, the Dominican Priory at the University of Paris, in 1245 to complete his novitiate and then to begin his study of philosophy and theology under the direction of Albert the following year.

The years Thomas spent first at Paris (1245–1248) and then at Cologne (1248–1252) as Albert's student gave him an excellent background in the thought of Aristotle, Pseudo-Dionysius, and Augustine, and prepared him well for his doctoral studies in theology at the University of Paris from 1252 to 1256. When Thomas finished his studies and became a Master of Theology in 1257 he understood his future responsibilities both as a Friar Preacher and a theologian very clearly. He believed he was called to preach the Gospel by explaining the truths of revelation contained in the Scriptures and the teachings of the church with the help of the insights of Aristotelian philosophy. In his teaching and writing Thomas sought to show that human life is the search to know experientially the God of infinite wisdom and love, who creates, sanctifies, and ultimately brings to fulfillment the whole of created reality in and through the life, death, and resurrection of Jesus Christ, who is truly God and truly human.

This vision would guide Thomas' teaching and writing in his years of service to the Order at various Dominican houses of study in Italy from 1259 to 1272, at St. Jacques upon his return to one of the Dominican chairs at the University of Paris from 1268 to 1272, and in his final years at the Dominican house of studies in Naples from 1272 to 1273. After a profound religious experience on December 6, 1273, Thomas ended his teaching and writing. He said: "Everything I have written seems like straw in comparison with what I have seen and what has been revealed to me." When this occurred he was in the midst of completing his theological masterpiece, the *Summa theologica,* and a shorter synopsis of his teaching, the *Compendium theologiae (Compendium of Theology).*

Thomas died a few months later on March 7, 1274 at the Cistercian Abbey of Fossanova, while traveling to the Second Council of Lyons. He was canonized by Pope John XXII in 1323. Pope Pius V declared him a doctor of the church in 1567. In 1880 Pope Leo XIII declared him the patron of all Catholic universities.

The *Summa theologica* is the most significant of the many writings of Thomas Aquinas. In this work he utilizes the framework of the Neoplatonic Augustinian tradition of the coming forth of creation from God *(exitus)* and the return of all things to God in Christ *(reditus).* Thomas' development of *exitus/reditus* is guided by four important perspectives.

1. The human person is a composite of body and soul that is directed toward a goal *(telos),* which is happiness. Human happiness is twofold. One is proportionate to our human nature, a happiness we can attain through habitual virtuous behavior, as Aristotle taught. The other is a happiness that surpasses human nature. We can obtain this happiness only by the gift of God's grace, which is a participation in God's own divine life. It is through Christ that we come to share in God's life through grace.

2. Grace builds on nature and restores what sin has wounded. Grace, as the gift of God, is a transformative quality or power that enables the human person to live in accord with God's will through the theological virtues of faith, hope, and love.

3. The Incarnation of the Divine Word, the second person of the blessed Trinity, manifests the immensity of God's love for human beings, wounded by sin. Christ, who is both truly divine and truly human, is the means of humanity's return to God through his life, death, and resurrection.

4. The sacraments, instituted by Christ as outward signs of inward grace, are the ordinary means by which God's grace is communicated to us.

The philosophical and theological perspectives that have stood at the heart of the Dominican tradition for nearly eight centuries flow from the fraternal and scholarly collaboration of Albert and Thomas as they sought to support the preaching mission of the Order through their study, teaching, and writing. The selections that follow are from Thomas' *Compendium of Theology.*

Thomas C. McGonigle, o.p.

From *Compendium of Theology*

1. Scope of the Present Work

To restore man, who had been laid low by sin, to the heights of divine glory, the Word of the eternal Father, though containing all things within His immensity, willed to become small. This He did, not by putting aside His greatness, but by taking to Himself our littleness. No one can say that he is unable to grasp the teaching of heavenly wisdom; what the Word taught at great length, although clearly, throughout the various volumes of Sacred Scripture for those who have leisure to study, He has reduced to brief compass for the sake of those whose time is taken up with the cares of daily life. Man's salvation consists in knowing the truth, so that the human mind may not be confused by diverse errors; in making for the right goal, so that man may not fall away from true happiness by pursuing wrong ends; and in carrying out the law of justice, so that he may not besmirch himself with a multitude of vices.

Knowledge of the truth necessary for man's salvation is comprised within a few brief articles of Faith. The Apostle says in Romans 9:28: "A short word shall the Lord make upon the Earth" and in a later passage he adds: "This is the word of faith, which we preach." In a short prayer Christ clearly marked out man's right course; and in teaching us to say this prayer, He showed us the goal of our striving and hope. In a single precept of charity He summed up that human justice which consists in observing the Law: "Love therefore is the fulfilling of the Law." Hence the Apostle taught that the whole perfection of this present life consists in faith, hope, and charity, as in certain brief headings outlining our salvation: "Now there remain faith, hope, and charity." These are the three virtues, as St. Augustine says, by which God is worshiped.

Wherefore, my dearest son Reginald, receive from my hands this compendious treatise on Christian teaching to keep continually before your eyes. My whole endeavor in the present work is taken up with these three virtues. I shall treat first of faith, then of hope, and lastly of charity. This is the Apostle's arrangement which, for that matter, right reason imposes. Love cannot be rightly ordered unless the proper goal of our hope is established; nor can there be any hope if knowledge of the truth is lacking. Therefore the first thing necessary is faith, by which you may come to a knowledge of the truth. Secondly, hope is necessary, that your intention may be fixed on the right end. Thirdly, love is necessary, that your affections may be perfectly put in order.

***

143. God's Special Providence Over Man by Grace

Accordingly, Divine Providence governs individual beings in keeping with their nature. Since rational creatures, because of the gift of free will, enjoy dominion over their actions in a way impossible to other creatures, a special Providence must be exercised over them in two respects: first, with regard to the aids God gives to rational creatures in their activity; secondly, with regard to the recompense allotted for their works. God gives to irrational creatures only those aids by which they are naturally moved to act. But to rational creatures are issued instructions and commands regulating their lives. A precept is not fittingly given except to a being that is master of his actions, although in an analogous sense God is said to give commands to irrational creatures also, as is intimated in Ps 148:6: "He hath made a decree, and it shall not pass away." But this sort of decree is nothing else than the dispensation of Divine Providence moving natural things to their proper actions.

The deeds of rational creatures are imputed to them in blame or in praise, because they have dominion over their acts. The actions of men are ascribed to them not only by a man who is placed over them, but also by God. Thus any praiseworthy or blameworthy action that a man performs is imputed to him by the person to whose rule he is subject. Since good actions merit a reward and sin calls for punishment, rational creatures are punished for the evil they do and are rewarded for the good they do, according to the measure of justice fixed by Divine Providence. But there is no place for reward or punishment in dealing with irrational creatures, just as there is none for praise or blame.

Since the last end of rational creatures exceeds the capacity of their nature and since whatever conduces to the end must be proportionate to the end according to the right order of Providence, rational creatures are given divine aids that are not merely proportionate to nature but that transcend the capacity of nature. God infuses into man, over and above the natural faculty of reason, the light of grace whereby he is internally perfected for the exercise of virtue, both as regards knowledge, inasmuch as man's mind is elevated by this light to the knowledge of truths surpassing reason, and as regards action and affection, inasmuch as man's affective power is raised by this light above all created things to the love of God, to hope in Him, and to the performance of acts that such love imposes.

These gifts or aids supernaturally given to man are called *graces* for two reasons. First, because they are given by God *gratis*. Nothing is discoverable in man that would constitute a right to aids of this sort, for they exceed the capacity of nature. Secondly, they are called *graces* because in a very special way, man is made *gratus* (or "pleasing to God") by such gifts. Since God's love is the cause of goodness in things and is not called forth by any preexisting goodness, as our love is, a special intensity of divine love must be discerned in those whom He showers with such extraordinary effects of His goodness. Therefore God is said chiefly and simply to love those whom He endows with these effects of His love by which they are enabled to reach their last end, which is He Himself, the fountainhead of all goodness.

144. Remission of Sin by the Gifts of Grace

Sins arise when actions deflect from the right course leading to the end. Since man is conducted to his end not only by natural aids, but by the aids of grace, the sins men commit must be counteracted not by natural aids alone, but also by the helps which grace confers. Contraries exclude each other; therefore, as the aids of grace are taken from man by sin, so sins are forgiven by the gifts of grace. Otherwise man's malice in committing sin would be more powerful in banishing divine grace than the divine goodness is in expelling sin by the gifts of grace.

Furthermore, God's Providence over things is in harmony with their mode of being. Changeable things are so constituted that contraries can succeed each other in them. Examples of this are generation and corruption in corporeal matter, and white and black in a colored object. Man is changeable in will as long as he lives his earthly life. Hence man receives from God the gifts of grace in such a way that he is able to forfeit them by sin; and the sins man commits are such that they can be remitted by the gifts of grace.

Besides, in supernatural acts, possible and impossible are regarded from the standpoint of divine power, not from the standpoint of natural power. The fact that a blind man can be made to see or that a dead man can rise, is owing not to natural power but to divine power. But the gifts of grace are supernatural. Therefore a person's capacity to receive them depends on divine power. To say that once a person has sinned he cannot receive the gifts of grace, is derogatory to the power of God. Of course, grace cannot coexist with sin; for by grace man is rightly ordered to his end, from which he is turned away by sin. But the contention that sin is irremissible impugns the power of God.

***

239. *The Twofold Life Restored in Man by Christ*

As Christ destroyed our death by His death, so He restored our life by His resurrection. Man has a twofold death and a twofold life. The first death is the death of the body, brought about by separation from the soul; the second death is brought about by separation from God. Christ, in whom the second death had no place, destroyed both of these deaths in us—that is, the bodily and the spiritual—by the first death He underwent (namely, that of the body).

Similarly, opposed to this twofold death we are to understand that there is a twofold life. One is a life of the body, imparted by the soul, and this is called the *life of nature*. The other comes from God and is called the *life of justice* or the *life of grace*. This life is given to us through faith, by which God dwells in us, according to Habakkuk 2:4: "The just shall live in his faith."

Accordingly, resurrection is also twofold: one is a bodily resurrection, in which the soul is united to the body for the second time; the other is a spiritual resurrection, in which the soul is again united to God. This second resurrection had no place in Christ, because His soul was never separated from God by sin. By His bodily resurrection, therefore, Christ is the cause of both the bodily and the spiritual resurrection in us.

However, as Augustine says in his commentary on St. John, we are to understand that the Word of God raises up souls but that the Word as incarnate raises up bodies. To give life to the soul belongs to God alone. Yet, since the flesh is the instrument of His divinity, and since an instrument operates in virtue of the principal cause, our double resurrection—bodily and spiritual—is referred to Christ's bodily resurrection as cause.

For everything done in Christ's flesh was salutary for us by reason of the divinity united to that flesh. Hence the Apostle, speaking of the resurrection of Christ as the cause of our spiritual resurrection, says, in Romans 4:25, that Christ "was delivered up for our sins and rose again for our justification." And in 1 Corinthians 15:12 he shows that Christ's resurrection is the cause of our bodily resurrection: "Now if Christ be preached, that He rose again from the dead, how do some among you say that there is no resurrection of the dead?"

Most aptly does the Apostle attribute remission of sins to Christ's death and our justification to His resurrection, thus tracing out conformity and likeness of effect to cause. As sin is discarded when it is remitted, so Christ by dying laid aside His Passible life, in which the likeness of sin was discernible. But when a person is justified, he receives new life. In like manner Christ, by rising, obtained newness of glory.

Therefore Christ's death is the cause of the remission of our sin: the efficient cause instrumentally, the exemplary cause sacramentally, and the meritorious cause. In like manner Christ's resurrection was also the cause of our resurrection: the efficient cause instrumentally and the exemplary cause sacramentally. But it was not a meritorious cause, for Christ was no longer a wayfarer, and so was not in a position to merit; and also because the glory of the Resurrection was the reward of His Passion, as the Apostle declares in Philippians 2:9ff.

Thus we see clearly that Christ can be called the first-born of those who rise from the dead. This is true not only in the order of time, inasmuch as Christ was the first to rise, as was said above, but also in the order of causality, because His resurrection is the cause of the resurrection of other men; and in the order of dignity, because He rose more gloriously than all others.

This belief in Christ's resurrection is expressed in the words of the Creed: "The third day He arose again from the dead."

***

4. Why We Must Pray to God for What We Hope

The reason why we must hope in God is chiefly the fact that we belong to Him, as effect belongs to cause. God does nothing in vain, but always acts for a definite purpose. Every active cause has the power of producing its effect in such a way that the effect will not be wanting in whatever can advance it toward its end. This is why, in effects produced by natural causes, nature is not found to be deficient in anything that is necessary, but confers on every effect whatever goes into its composition and is required to carry through the action whereby it may reach its end. Of course, some impediment may arise from a defect in the cause, which then may be unable to furnish all this.

A cause that operates intellectually not only confers on the effect, in the act of producing it, all that is required for the result intended, but also, when the product is finished, controls its use, which is the end of the object. Thus a smith, in addition to forging a knife, has the disposition of its cutting efficiency. Man is made by God somewhat as an article is made by an artificer. Something of this sort is said in Isaiah 64:8: "And now, O Lord, Thou art our Father and we are clay, and Thou art our Maker."

Accordingly, just as an earthen vessel, if it were endowed with sense, might hope to be put to good use by the potter, so man ought to cherish the hope of being rightly provided for by God. Thus we are told in Jeremiah 18:6: "As clay is in the hand of the potter, so are you in my hand, O house of Israel."

The confidence which man has in God ought to be most certain. As we just intimated, a cause does not refrain from rightly controlling its product unless it labors under some defect. But no defect or ignorance can occur in God because "all things are naked and open to His eyes," as is said in Hebrews 4:13. Nor does He lack power, for "the hand of the Lord is not shortened that it cannot save," as we read in Isaiah 59:1. Nor is He wanting in good will, for "the Lord is good to them that hope in Him, to the soul that seeketh Him," as we are reminded in Lamentations 3:25. Therefore the hope with which a person trusts in God does not confound him that hopes, as is said in Romans 5:5.

We should also bear in mind that, while Providence watches solicitously over all creatures, God exercises special care over rational beings. For the latter are exalted to the dignity of God's image, and can rise to the knowledge and love of Him, and have dominion over their actions, since they are able to discriminate between good and evil. Hence they should have confidence in God, not only that they may be preserved in existence in keeping with the condition of their nature—for this pertains also to other creatures—but that, by avoiding evil and doing good, they may merit some reward from Him. We are taught a salutary lesson in Psalm 35:7: "Men and beasts Thou wilt preserve" (that is, God bestows on men and irrational creatures alike whatever pertains to the sustaining of life). And then the Psalmist adds, in the next verse: "But the children of men shall put their trust under the covert of Thy wings," indicating that they will be protected by God with special care.

We should observe, further, that when any perfection is conferred, an ability to do or acquire something is also added. For example, when the air is illuminated by the sun, it has the capacity to serve as a medium for sight; and when water is heated by fire it can be used to cook—and it could hope for this if it had a mind. To man is given, over and above the nature of his soul, the perfection of grace, by which he is made a partaker in the divine nature, as we are taught in 2 Peter 1:4. As a result of this, we are said to be regenerated and to become sons of God, according to John 1:12. "He gave them power to be made the sons of God." Thus raised to be sons, men may reasonably hope for an inheritance, as we learn from Romans 8:17: "If sons, heirs also." In keeping with this spiritual regeneration, man should have a yet higher hope in God, namely, the hope of receiving an eternal inheritance, according to 1 Peter 1:3-4: "God . . . hath regenerated us unto a lively hope, by the resurrection of Jesus Christ from the dead, unto an inheritance incorruptible, undefiled, and which cannot fade, reserved in Heaven for you."

Through this "spirit of adoption" that we receive, we cry: "*Abba* (Father)," as is said in Romans 8:15. Hence our Lord began His prayer by calling upon the Father, saying, "Father," to teach us that our prayer must be based on this hope. By uttering the name, "Father," man's affection is prepared to pray with a pure disposition, and also to obtain what he hopes for. Moreover, sons ought to be imitators of their parents. Therefore he who professes that God is his Father ought to try to be an imitator of God, by avoiding things that make him unlike God and by earnestly praying for those perfections that make him like to God. Hence we are commanded in Jeremiah 3:19: "Thou shalt call me *Father* and shalt not cease to walk after me."

Mechtild of Magdeburg (1208–1282/1294)

The exact circumstances of the birth of the woman now known as Mechtild of Magdeburg are shrouded in the humbling veil of lost history. She possibly or even probably was born to a lesser noble family in about 1208 in the region now known as Saxony-Anhalt in Germany, within the territory then comprising the Archdiocese of Magdeburg. Her exact date of death is fixed variously at 1282, 1285, and around 1294, depending on interpretation of internal documentation of the seven books of her *The Flowering Light of the Godhead*. She died at the Cistercian monastery of Helfta, near Eisleben. While she was not formally a Dominican, she is remembered as a mystic steeped in Dominican spirituality and can stand here as representative of the thousands of unknown Dominican nuns and Third Order members, as well as the many Beguines (the terms perhaps come from the old Flemish *beghen*, "to pray") who joined Dominican convents and bore anonymous witness to Dominic's vision.

Magdeburg, situated along the Elbe River, was among the most important merchant cities in medieval Europe. Growing up in its environs, Mechtild must have known the growing importance of Magdeburg as a center of trade and politics. In the thirteenth century the city gave its name to the Magdeburg Rights and was among the first to join the Hanseatic League.

Mechtild reports that at the age of twelve she began to receive regular graces—she calls them "greetings" of the Holy Spirit—that continued for thirty years. Magdeburg's trade relations to the west, as far as Flanders, may have brought the flourishing Beguine movement closer to her, for around 1230 when she was in her early twenties she began to live as a Beguine at Magdeburg. As she lived the apostolic life of a Beguine, perhaps ministering to the sick, preparing the dead for burial, and earning a simple living by handwork, her visions continued. Her confessor and spiritual director, the Dominican Heinrich of Halle, directed her to write them down, which she did beginning around 1250. Mechtild reports that God dictated the title of the book as *"Lessened light miner goethite in all die herein die ad lambent anew vastest,"* i.e., "Light of my divinity, flowing into all hearts that live without guile." She wrote on separate folios and gave each to Heinrich of Halle. She completed the sixth volume in 1264.

But by what right did she write? She was untutored in theology and belonged to no approved religious order. Worse, she belonged to a movement widely criticized and beyond the control of ecclesiastical authority. Various slanders were directed at the Beguines in general and endangered even Mechtild. Local synods in Germany during her time attacked the movement, and one held in Magdeburg in 1261 specifically ordered Beguines, under penalty of excommunication, to obey their parish priests. What she said, and especially what she was writing, seems to have circulated beyond the safety of her inner circle of friends. She appears to have been criticized, but she persevered. She writes:

> I was warned about this book and told by many
> That it should not be preserved
> But rather thrown into the flames . . . (II:26).

Mechtild wrote confidently, but her outspokenness—particularly regarding the vices of the clergy both in general and in Magdeburg—soon led her to seek shelter among the Cistercian nuns at Helfta, not far from Magdeburg, in about 1270. She never became a Cistercian, but the Abbess, Gertrude of Hakeborn (1231–1290) allowed her to live in the community for the rest of her life. The writings of two Cistercians at Helfta, Mechtild of Hackeborn (1241–1299), and Gertrude the Great (1256–1302), show the influence of Mechtild's words.

Mechtild continued her written work, now known as *The Flowing Light of the Godhead* ("*Das fliessende Licht der Gottheit*"), adding the seventh and final volume at Helfta. She wrote in Middle Low German (German of the middle period, 1050–1450, and of the low or northern geographical area), but that manuscript is considered irrevocably lost. A translation of the first six volumes from Middle Low German to Latin made in 1290 by a Dominican is reprinted, along with a translation of the seventh volume, in *Revelationes Gertrudianse ac Mechtildianae II* (Paris, 1877), 435–707.

Hence what we have in English are translations of translations made well after Mechtild wrote. The selections below are translated from the Middle High (southern) German translation of Heinrich of Nördlingen around 1344, now known as the Einsiedeln Manuscript (Codex 277). Nördlingen, who was in contact with John Tauler and perhaps with Henry Suso, and advisor to several convents, complained about the strangeness of Mechtild's German.

Mechtild's writings about purgatory depict grades or levels, the lowest the most torturous and the highest not far from heaven, and her depiction of the hereafter seems to be a basis for Dante's *Divine Comedy*. Dante's Matilda (*Purgatory*, Cantos 27–33) seems to be identical to Mechtild.

While Mechtild has not been canonized, she is venerated among the great Rhineland mystics, including and especially the two other medieval mystics of Helfta, Gertrude the Great and Mechtild of Hakeborn. In the selections from her writings below she introduces both herself and her book, in which she later discusses the Order of Preachers. The final selection, near the end of her writings, presents "the simplicity of love."

Phyllis Zagano

From *The Flowering Light of the Godhead*

26. Of This Book and Its Writer

> I was warned about this book and told by many
> That is should not be preserved
> But rather thrown to the flames.
> > Then did I what from childhood I have done
> When trouble overcame me:
> I betook myself to prayer.
> I bowed myself to my Love and said:
> "Lord! now am I troubled:
> Must I walk uncomforted for Thy Glory?
> Thou hast misled me
> For Thou Thyself commandest me to write!"
> > Then God showed Himself to my weary soul
> And holding the book in His right hand He said:
> "Beloved! Fret not thyself too sore!
> The Truth may no man burn.

Those who would take this book out of My hand
Must be stronger than I!
This book is threefold
And concerns Me alone.
The parchment here before Me
Deals with My pure, righteous and wise humanity
Which suffered death for thee.
The words denote My glorious Divinity
Which flows from hour to hour
Into thy soul from My Divine mouth.
The voice of the words denotes My Living Spirit
And fulfils in itself the living Truth.
    Now see in all these words
How praisefully they proclaim My holiness
And doubt not thyself!"

    "Ah! Lord! were I a learned priest
And hadst Thou worked this wonder in him
Then hadst Thou endless honour therefrom.
    But how can any believe
That on this unworthy soil
Thou couldst raise up a golden house
And live therein with Thy mother
And all creatures
And all the heavenly host?
Lord! Therein can I find no earthly wisdom!"
    "Daughter! Many a wise man loses his precious gold
Carelessly on the great highway
  On which he would come to the upper school;
But someone must find it!
I have long acted thus:
Wherever I gave special grace
I sought for the lowest and smallest and most hidden.
  The highest mountains may not receive
  The revelations of My Grace,
For the flood of My Holy Spirit
Flows by nature down into the valleys.
    One finds many a wise writer of books
Who in himself, to My sight, is a fool.
And I tell thee further, it greatly honours Me
  And strengthens mightily Holy Church
That unlearned lips should teach

The learned tongues of My Holy Spirit."
Ah! Lord! I sigh and long and pray for Thy
scribe
Who has copied this book for me,
That Thou wouldst reward him also
With grace never granted to man;
For Thy Grace, O Lord, is a thousandfold more
Than Thy creatures can ever receive!

Then spake our Lord:
"He has written it in letters of gold,
Therefore shall every word of it
Be inscribed on his cloak
In gleaming, heavenly gold:
For pure love must ever be
The highest of all human attributes."

When the Lord said these words to me
I saw the glorious Truth in eternal merit:
Ah! Lord! I pray Thee preserve this book
From the eyes of the false
Who come from nether regions, never from above.
For they are conceived in Lucifer's heart
Born in spiritual pride, reared in hatred,
And grown up in scorn without virtue.
God's children must suffer from this
And be oppressed by such ignominy
If with Jesus they would receive the highest honour.
We must ever keep a holy watchfulness on ourselves
And on our even-Christians,
So that should they err we may faithfully warn them
And thus save ourselves many unnecessary words.

Amen

***

27. Of the End of the Order of Preachers; of Anti-Christ, Elias and Enoch (Condensed)

The Order of Preachers was bitterly assailed by false masters and by jealous sinners. Therefore I begged our Lord to protect His honour in the Order. He spoke: "So long as I desire it, no one can destroy it." I asked: "Shall the Order continue to the end of the world?" Our Lord said: "Yes . . . but others like it shall come. They will be poorer in earthly desires and more filled with the fire of the Holy Spirit through the great need in which Holy Church will then be." Then I saw those others and their kind of life. . . .

They had only two garments, the under was white and the upper red, signifying the pure humanity of our Lord and His holy death. Their girdles were made from the bast of an olive tree to signify the compassion they bore to orphaned Christianity. They all go barefoot: when it freezes they wear red shoes with white laces but no stockings. . . . They have no dwellings of their own. They are strangers in every city and suffer many hardships. . . . Each carries a staff; it is coloured white and red; it has a cross-piece one span long and is made of ivory, signifying that the brethren are pure in all things. . . . On one side of the staff is carved the crucifixion; on the other the Ascension. The brethren must have this staff with them everywhere. . . . When they let it out of their hands, they must drive it into the ground, that they may always look on the cross. If the distance they must travel is thirty miles, then . . . every two must take a donkey on which each may ride for a stretch. Their staff must be held erect in their hands as a cross. They must ride that humble beast that they may be like our Lord in humility, also because otherwise their feet would be so sore that they could not make long journeys. . . . They shall not ask for books or clothes. But where bread is not offered, they must humbly ask for it; they shall eat and drink with the people any food they are offered, except only meat. They shall not fast more than Church law ordains and shall seek shelter away from others that they may pray and sleep under a separate roof.

When the people recognize this holy life, they will be so edified thereby that they will gladly supply its needs. The people will wash the hardened feet of the brethren with fervour, and will thank God that they thus travel about ministering to orphaned Christianity as Mary Magdalene did.

***

43. Of the Simplicity of Love

> Those who would know much but love little
> Ever remain at the beginning of a good life.
> Therefore we should ever carry awe in our hearts
> If we would inwardly please God.

For simple love even with little knowledge
Work great things within.
Holy simplicity is the way to all wisdom:
It shows the wise they are but fools,
For when simplicity of heart
Lives in the wisdom of the senses
Much holiness comes to the human soul.

Meister Eckhart (c. 1260–c. 1329)

Johann Eckhart was born about 1260 at Hochheim on the River Main, near Gotha, and died in 1329 at Cologne. Although he is remembered as a "Master" *(Meister)*, the teachings of this Dominican preacher, theologian, and mystic were questioned in his life and remain problematic today. His nontechnical approach to doctrine caused both the learned and the unlearned to misunderstand his teachings and intent. The central doctrinal concern is Eckhart's failure to integrate his theology of God's essence and of God's manifestation. The fact that he did not systematize his image theology makes Eckhart controversial to this day, even as he is known as the father of German mysticism.

Eckhart entered the Dominican priory at Erfurt as a youth and studied philosophy and theology at the Dominican *studium generale* for advanced studies at Cologne. He also studied at Paris in 1296, reading Peter Lombard's *Sentences.* He was both a talented scholar and a good administrator. By 1298 he was elected prior at Erfurt and vicar-provincial of Thuringia. He was twice elected provincial of the province of Saxony, and was also appointed vicar-general of Bohemia in 1307 with a mandate of reform. He taught for two years at Paris, where like Thomas Aquinas he held the Dominican chair of philosophy, until he moved in 1314 to Strasbourg. In 1317 he became prior at Frankfurt, but returned to teaching in 1324 and was made first professor of his Order at Cologne.

Eckhart is known primarily as a preacher, both in speech and in writing. His style made the substance of his work attractive and understandable although his own intellectual and mystical depth often ran ahead of that of his listeners and interlocutors. Eckhart's main themes are the divine essence, the relationship between God and humans, and the operations of the soul. He was less a philosopher than a master of spiritual theology; although his doctrine did follow that of Albert and Aquinas, he did not employ scholastic style or logic. Recent scholarship tends to argue that his thought more followed Augustine than deviated from that of Aquinas. His writings definitely display a Neoplatonist influence, and his late Augustinianism follows the work of Hugh of St. Victor.

Eckhart began his life and work in Germany not far from Mechthild of Magdeburg, although it is unknown whether she or her writings influenced him. He did directly influence John Tauler and Henry Suso, both Dominicans and mystics, and he held high status and had a large following during his lifetime. In 1329 the papal condemnation of twenty-eight of his propositions effectively ended that fame and support. He was not condemned by the Spanish Jesuits in 1575, as were Tauler and Ruusbroec, but neither was he widely known until the mid-nineteenth century, when selections from his German works were published in Austria.

Eckhart's century was at once filled with and harsh on both Beghards and Beguines, who were accused of any number of errors including quietism and pantheism. While some of their number did hold erroneous doctrine, the groups were perhaps most seriously guilty of not being within the direct control of clergy. Controversy followed Eckhart wherever he went, and early in 1327 the Archbishop of Cologne undertook an independent inquiry so damaging that Eckhart denied the misinterpretation of his work and retracted any possible errors, submitting to the judgment of the Holy See, all of which was published in the Bull *Dolentes referimus* (27 March 1329) of Pope John XXII, in which seventeen of his propositions were deemed heretical and eleven possibly heretical. That said, not all of Eckhart's work has survived, so it is impossible to form a correct judgment on the doctrinal truth or falsity of what he actually said and wrote.

The key to Eckhart's doctrine is the ontological argument that only God "exists." That is, his philosophy of Being argues that all except God lacks substantial essence. Hence creatures may possess being, but God *is* Being. Finally, he argues that God is the essence of Being, for if God is the cause of Being, God must transcend Being. Thereby the true nature of God is "thinking" or "knowing" or "understanding," which is primacy. The human capacity for self-reflective consciousness flows from God and participates in God, as the "spark of the soul." In the context of his day, with complaints of pantheism knocking at the doors of Beghards and Beguines, it is easy to understand how his failure to present a clear division between the Creator and the created could be interpreted as nonorthodox. How he failed to be alert to the possibilities of misinterpretation is a mystery, although, as Oliver Davies has pointed out, the combination of his high academic status and his mystical experience of God may have contributed to his often incautious language.[1] That is, were his words coming only from a mystic, they could have been understood as such. But Eckhart was also a priest and academic, and his teaching authority caused his writing to be scrutinized more carefully, and to be misunderstood.

There are a number of contemporary translations of Eckhart's works. Perhaps those in widest circulation are in the Classics in Western Spirituality series (Paulist Press), from which the following excerpt is taken.

Phyllis Zagano

From *Sermon 30: Praedica verbum, vigila, in omnibus labora (2 Tm. 4:2)*

One reads a phrase today and tomorrow concerning my master St. Dominic. St. Paul writes it in the epistle and in German it means: "Speak the word, speak it externally, speak it forth, bring it forth, give birth to the Word!"

It is a marvelous thing that something flows out yet remains within. That a word flows out yet remains within is certainly marvelous. That all creatures flow out yet remain within is a wonder. What God has given and what he has promised to give is simply marvelous, incomprehensible, unbelievable. And this is as it should be; for if it were intelligible and believable, it would not be right. God is in all things. The more he is in things, the more he is outside the things; the more within; the more outside; the more outside, the more within. I have said many times that God creates the whole world right now all at once. All that God created six thousand years ago and earlier when God made the world—all this he is creating now completely. God is in all things; but God as divine and God as intelligent is nowhere so intensely present as he is in the soul and in the angels; if you will, in the innermost and in the highest [part] of the soul. And when I say "the innermost," I mean the

1. *The Rhineland Mystics: Writings of Meister Eckhart, Johannes Tauler, and Jan van Ruusbroec and Selections from the* Theologia Germanica *and the* Book of Spiritual Poverty. Edited by Oliver Davies. New York: Crossroad, 1990.

highest; and when I say "the highest," I mean the innermost of the soul. In the innermost and in the highest of the soul: I mean them both in one. There, where time never entered nor image shined in, in this innermost and highest [part] of the soul, God creates this whole world. Everything that God created six thousand years ago when he made the world and everything he will yet create in a thousand years (if the world lasts that long), all this he creates in the innermost and in the highest of the soul. Everything that is past, everything that is present, and everything that is future God creates in the innermost of the soul. Everything that God accomplishes in all the saints he accomplishes in the innermost of the soul. The Father gives birth to his Son in the innermost of the soul and gives birth to you with his only-begotten Son, not less. If I am to be the Son, I have to be the Son in the same being in which he is the Son and in no other. If I am to be human, I cannot be a man in the being of an animal; I have to be a man in the being of a man. But if I am to be *this* man, I have to be this man in *this* being. Now St. John says, "You are children of God" (Cf. 1 Jn. 3:1).

"Speak the word, speak it externally, speak it forth, bring it forth, give birth to the Word!" "Speak it externally." That something is spoken from the outside in is a common thing. This, however, is spoken within. "Speak it externally!" This means: Be aware that this is within you. The prophet says, "God spoke one thing, and I heard two" (Cf. Ps. 61:12). This is true. God has only ever spoken one thing. His speech is only one. In this one speaking he speaks his Son and, together with him, the Holy Spirit and all creatures; and there is only one speaking in God. But the prophet says, "I heard two," that is, I understood God and creatures. Where God speaks it, it is God; but here it is creature. People imagine that God only became man there [in Palestine]. This is not true. God has just as much become man here [in the soul] as there, and he has become man so that he might give birth to you, his only-begotten Son, and nothing less.

I was sitting someplace yesterday when I spoke a phrase from the "Our Father," which says, "Your will be done!" (Mt. 6:10). But it would be better thus: "May will become yours," [in the sense] that my will becomes his will, that I become he: This is the meaning of the *Pater Noster.* The phrase has two meanings. The first is: Sleep [unaware] of all things; that is, that you know nothing about time or creatures or images. The masters say: If a person were really asleep for a hundred years, he would not know any creature and he would not know of time or images. [Only if you so sleep,] then you can hear what God is bringing about in you. This is why the soul says in the Book of Love: "I sleep and my heart is awake" (Sg. 5:2). Therefore, if all creatures are asleep in you, you can become aware of what God is bringing about in you.

The phrase "Work in all things" (2 Tm. 4:5) contains three meanings. It is the same as if to say: Achieve your advantage in all things; which is: Take God in all things because God is in all things. St. Augustine says: "God created all things, not by letting them come about and then going on his way; rather, he remained in them." People imagine that they have more if they have both things and God than if they have God but not things. But this is wrong because all things together with God are not more than God by himself. And if someone who had both Father and Son in him were to think that he had more than if he had the Son but not the Father, he would be wrong. For the Father together with the Son is not more than the Son by himself, and the Son with the Father is not more than the Father by himself. Therefore, take God in all things in this manner, and that is a sign that he has given birth to you, his only-begotten Son, and nothing less.

The second meaning of "achieve your advantage in all things" is: "Love God above all things and your neighbor as yourself" (Lk. 10:27), and this is a command from God. But I say that it is not just a commandment; rather, it is also what God has given and what he has promised to give. And if you love your own hundred marks more than someone else's, this is wrong. If you like one person more than another, this is wrong. If you like your father, your mother, and yourself more than some other person, this is wrong. [Someone might say:] "My goodness! What are you saying? Should I not prefer my own happiness to that of another person?" There are many learned people who do not understand this and think it terribly difficult, yet it is not difficult but very easy. I shall show you that it is not difficult. Look! Nature has two purposes which each part of a human being pursues in its works, namely, that is serve the body as a whole and, secondly, [that it serve] each part [of the body] separately for that part's good not less than for its own good. But it [each part] does not consider itself more in its works than some other part. How much more must this be true in the realm of grace. God should be the measure and the foundation of your love. The first intention of your love should be purely God and then your neighbor as yourself and not less than yourself. And if you love happiness more in yourself than in someone else, this is wrong. For if you love happiness in yourself more than in someone else, you [really just] love yourself; and where you love yourself, there God is not purely your love, and this is then wrong. If you like happiness in St. Peter and St. Paul as much as in yourself, you possess the same happiness which they also have. And if you like happiness in the angels as much as in yourself and if you like happiness in our Lady as much as in yourself, you enjoy the very same happiness that she does. It is yours as genuinely as hers. Thus one says in the Book of Wisdom, "He made him like his saints" (Cf. Si. 45:2).

The third meaning of "achieve your advantage in all things" is: Love God equally in all things. This means: Love God as much in poverty as in wealth; care for him as much in sickness as in health. Love him as much when being tried as when not, and as much in suffering as when free of suffering. Truly, the more the suffering, the less the suffering; like two buckets: the heavier the one, the lighter the other. The more a person renounces, the easier he finds it to renounce. A person who loves God would find it as easy to give up this whole world as [he would to give up] an egg. The more he renounces, the easier it is for him to renounce. This was the case with the apostles. The worse their sufferings were, the more easily they suffered.

"Work in all things!" (2 Tm. 4:5). This means: Whenever you find yourself in various kinds of things and not in bare, pure, simple being, let this be your work: "Work in all things, completing your service" (2 Tm. 4:5). This means: Lift up your head. And this has two meanings. First, put everything aside that is yours and lay claim to God. Then God will be your own as he is his own very own. He will be God for you as he is God for himself, and not less. What is mine I do not have from anyone. But if I have it from someone else, it is not mine but rather his from whom I have it. The other meaning of "lift up your head" is: Direct all your works to God. There are many people who do not understand this, and this seems to me hardly surprising. For the person who is to understand this must be totally detached and elevated above all things.

That we may arrive at such perfection, may God help us.

Amen.

Catherine of Siena (1347–1380)

Caterina di Giacomo di Benincasa was born twenty-fourth of her parents' twenty-five children in the medieval walled city of Siena. While the modern mind sees Siena as about one hour from Florence and three hours from Rome by car, fourteenth-century Siena was a world unto itself. The bustling city was reflected within the grounds of her father's house and property; all manner of distraction awaited the little twin, Caterina.

But at the age of seven Catherine vowed herself to Christ. At fifteen she cut her hair in defiance of her parents' plans for her marriage, and at eighteen she became a Dominican tertiary. For the ensuing three years she led a silent life in a small stone room in her father's house, later reporting regular mystical experiences and conversations with Christ. Possibly during the Siena Carnival of 1368, Catherine mystically experienced her spiritual espousal to Christ. The spiritual marriage was apparently acknowledged by Catherine's contemporaries and was artistically recorded about one hundred twenty years later in two famous paintings, *The Marriage of Saint Catherine of Siena* (c. 1481–1500) by Lorenzo d'Alessandro da Sanseverino, now at the National Gallery, London, and the Florentine Dominican Fra Bartolomeo's *The Mystic Marriage of St. Catherine of Siena, with Eight Saints* (1511), which hangs in the Louvre, besides many lesser works.

So claimed by Christ at twenty-one, Catherine began to live a more active, or apostolic, life. She tended the ill and the poor of Siena and worked for the conversion of those who had turned from Christ and the church. She was well known and well regarded by the people of Siena, and soon attracted a following of women and men.

In 1370 Catherine received a vision of the end of life as heaven, purgatory, and hell. She left her stable life of prayer and service, anchored as it was in her little cell, for an even more public ministry. She wrote letters to all manner of powerful persons—princes of the various republics of Italy, papal legates, and anyone else who could address the raging upheavals of her day. In 1375 she received the stigmata, the wounds of which (at her request) did not appear during her lifetime. As factions continued to arise, and war simmered and boiled between neighboring Florence and the Holy See, Catherine secured the neutrality of Pisa and Lucca and unsuccessfully attempted to end the fighting during a June 1376 visit to Pope Gregory XI, in exile at Avignon. While her direct mission failed, Catherine made such an impression on Gregory that he ended the Avignon papacy and returned to Rome six months later, despite the measured opposition of the French King and of the College of Cardinals. Not incidentally, Catherine also made pointed public and private requests for the reform of the clergy and the proper administration of the Papal States.

Catherine's personal privations were echoed by her physical asceticism; she lived in the constant physical and social pain of her unseen stigmata. Even so, she remained unfailingly cheerful, especially during her times of persecution by men and women Dominicans.

Early in 1378 Catherine went to Florence as the Pope's emissary, again in an effort to restore the peace. Her attempted assassination during a small popular uprising was foiled, and she internalized her survival as God's withdrawal of the "red rose of martyrdom" because of her sins. Later that year, as warfare ended, Catherine returned to Siena, where she dictated her "Dialogue." She longed to return to Rome, and did so late that year, praying daily at St. Peter's Basilica. By 1380 she could no longer eat, and she became bedridden two months prior to her death on April 29, which date is now celebrated as her feast day. She is patron of Italy and of Europe.

Catherine wrote hundreds of letters in addition to her major work, *The Dialogue of Saint Catherine of Siena,* also known as *A Treatise on Divine Providence.* Catherine's *Dialogue* was newly divided by Professor Giuliana Cavallini in 1968, and the selections that follow come from the Suzanne Noffke translation of that work, as well as from her translation of Cavallini's book of *The Prayers of Catherine of Siena.* Along with *The Life of Catherine of Siena* by her confessor and spiritual director, Dominican Raymond of Capua, these combine to tell the phenomenal story of a soul captured by God.

Both truth and love are central to Catherine's thought and mysticism. God is truth, and God is love. Throughout the *Dialogue* there is a recurring pattern of petition, answer, and thanksgiving as the soul entreats God for a better understanding of truth so that she might love more. As Cavallini points out, "This thread running throughout the book is the theme of truth fostering love, which is fully developed under the image of Christ-the-bridge, whose ascent is a progress to the perfection of love—which is the perfection of human nature."[1]

Catherine's four petitions in the *Dialogue* are (1) for herself, to be able to love better; (2) for the reform of the church; (3) for the whole world, and especially for peace; (4) for divine providence in all things. The central part of the *Dialogue* presents a metaphor of Christ as the bridge to the knowledge of God (perhaps taken from Gregory the Great, but fully developed by Catherine). Later Catherine asks the Lord for understanding of tears, the means by which the soul passes through the stages explained by the bridge. Later, in a further development of the metaphor of the bridge, Catherine understands the three lights of human knowledge: the imperfect (refusal to judge others' vices), the perfect (refusal to judge others' degree of perfection), and the most perfect (refusal to demand all follow the same way), each of which move the soul to truth.

The selections that follow are a summary of God's explanations of tears to Catherine, and three sections that delineate her understanding of truth.

Phyllis Zagano

From *The Dialogue*

90

> Now you have seen the different kinds of tears and the differences among them, as it has pleased my truth to satisfy your desire.
>
> The first kind of tears, the tears of those who are dead in sin, come from a heart that is corrupt. Now the heart is the source of all emotion, which in turn is the source of tears. So because these persons' heart is corrupt, the weeping that comes from it is corrupt and wretched, and so are all their actions.
>
> The second kind of weeping is that of souls who are beginning to know their own sinfulness through the punishment that must be their lot after sinning. This is a common sort of beginning that I in

1. *Catherine of Siena: The Dialogue*, tr. Suzanne Noffke. Preface by Giuliana Cavallini (New York: Paulist, 1980) xv.

my kindness grant to weak souls who like fools are drowning down there in the river because they shun my Truth's teaching. There are so very many who come as far as this sort of self-knowledge. Without slavish fear of their own punishment they would perish. Some, in a sudden great contempt for themselves, come to consider themselves deserving of punishment. There are others who give themselves in wholesome simplicity to serving me their Creator because they are sorry they have offended me. Those who go the way of great self-contempt are, it is true, more apt to reach perfection than the others. Both will reach it if they exert themselves, but the former will get there sooner. The first sort must take care not to rest in their slavish fear. The others must watch out for tepidity, for if they do not exercise their simplicity it will grow lukewarm within them. This is an ordinary sort of calling.

The third and fourth kinds of weeping belong to those who have risen above fear and attained to love and hope. They taste my divine mercy and receive from me many gifts and consolations, and because of these things their eyes, responding to the heart's emotion, weep. This weeping is still imperfect, because it is mixed with weeping that is spiritually sensual. But if these souls exercise themselves in virtue they reach the fourth stage, where, because their desire has grown, they so unite themselves with my will that they can no longer desire anything but what I will. They are clothed with a charity for their neighbors that gives birth in them to a lover's lament that I am offended and their neighbors hurt.

Such weeping is one with the fifth sort, that of ultimate perfection. Here the soul is united with Truth and the flame of holy desire burns more fiercely within her. The devil flees from this desire and can no longer persecute the soul—not by assaulting her, because love for her neighbors has made her patient, nor by using spiritual or temporal consolations, because she would spurn such things in contempt and true humility.

It is indeed true that the devil never sleeps but teaches you, if you are careless, to sleep when it is profitable to him. But his watching cannot hurt these perfect souls, for he cannot stand the heat of their charity, nor the fragrance of their soul's union with me, the sea of peace. No, the soul cannot be tricked so long as she remains united with me. So the devil flees like a fly from a boiling caldron, because he is afraid of the fire. If the soul were lukewarm he would enter fearlessly—though often enough he perishes there when he finds it hotter than he had imagined! So it happens with the soul when she first reaches perfection. The devil comes in, because she seems to him to be lukewarm, with different sorts of temptations. But if the soul has the least bit of knowledge and heat and hatred of sin, she resists him, binding her will steadfast with the chains of hatred for sin and love for virtue.

Let every soul rejoice who suffers many troubles, because such is the road that leads to this delightfully glorious state. I have told you before that you reach perfection through knowledge and contempt of yourself and knowledge of my goodness. And at no time does the soul know herself so well, if I am within her, as when she is most beleaguered. Why? I will tell you. She knows herself well when she finds herself besieged and can neither free herself nor resist being captured. Yes, she can resist with her will to the point of not giving her consent, but that is all. *Then* she can come to know that [of herself] she is nothing. For if she were anything at all of herself, she would be able to get rid of what she did not want. So in this way she is humbled in true self-knowledge, and in the light of holy faith she runs to me, God eternal. For by my kindness she was able to maintain her good and holy will steadfast when she was sorely besieged, so that she did not imitate the wretched things that were vexing her.

You have good reason, then, to take comfort in the teaching of the gentle loving Word, my only-begotten Son, in times of great trouble, suffering, and adversity, and when you are tempted by people or the devil. For these things strengthen your virtue and bring you to great perfection.

***

98

That soul's hunger and thirst, her sincerity and the longing with which she asked to be able to serve him pleased God eternal. So he looked on her with compassionate mercy and said:

O dearest daughter whom I so love, you who are my bride, rise above yourself and open your mind's eye. Look at me, infinite Goodness, and see my unspeakable love for you and my other servants. And open the sensitive ear of your desire. This is the only way you will see and hear, for the soul who does not have my Truth for the object of her mind's eye can neither hear nor know my truth. Therefore I want you to rise above your senses so that you may more surely know the truth. Then I will satisfy you, for I am pleased with your desire and your questioning. Not that you can increase my pleasure: It is I who make you grow, not you me. But the very pleasure I take in my creation pleases me.

So that soul obeyed. She rose above herself to know the truth about what she had asked. Then God eternal said to her:

So that you may better understand what I am about to tell you, let me begin at the source of the answer: the three lights that come forth from me, the true Light.

The first is an ordinary light in those whose charity is ordinary. (I will repeat what I have already told you about this, that, and many other things even though you have already heard them, so that your meager understanding may better comprehend what I want you to know.) The other two lights belong to those who have risen above the world and are seeking perfection. Beyond this I shall explain what you have asked me to, being more specific about what I have already touched on more broadly.

You know that no one can walk in the way of truth without the light of reason that you draw from me, the true Light, through the eye of your understanding. You must have as well the light of faith, which you possess as my gift from holy baptism unless you have put it out with your sins. In baptism, through the power of my only-begotten Son's blood, you received the form of faith. If you exercise this faith by virtue with the light of reason, reason will in turn be enlightened by faith, and such faith will give you life and lead you in the way of truth. With this light you will reach me, the true Light; without it you would come to darkness.

There are two lights drawn from this [first] light that you must have, and to the two I will add yet a third.

The first is that you must all be enlightened to know the transitory things of this world, that they all pass away like the wind. But you cannot know this well unless you first know your own weakness, how ready that perverse law bound up in your members makes you to rebel against me your Creator. Not that this law can force any one of you to commit the least sin unless you want to, but it certainly does fight against the spirit. Nor did I give this law so that my people should be conquered, but so that they might increase and prove virtue in their souls. For virtue can be proved only by its opposite. Sensuality is the opposite of the spirit, so it is through sensuality that the soul proves the love she has for me her Creator. When does she prove it? When she mounts hatred and contempt against it.

I gave the soul this law also to keep her truly humble. So you see, while I created her in my image and likeness and made her so honorable and beautiful, I gave her as well the vilest thing there is, this perverse law. In other words, I bound her into a body formed from the vilest earth so that when she saw her beauty she would not lift up her head in pride against me. So the weak body is a reason for humility to those who have this light [of mine]. They have no reason at all to be proud, but they do have reason for true and perfect humility. This perverse law, then, no matter how it fights, cannot force the least sin. Rather it is reason for you to learn to know yourself and to know how inconstant is the world.

The eye of understanding ought to see this through the light of holy faith, which is that eye's pupil. This is that essential light which everyone in every situation must have to share in the life of grace, in the fruit of the spotless Lamb's blood. This is the ordinary light, and everyone must have it. Those who do not have it are damned. Because they do not have the light they are not living in grace, for without the light they do not recognize the evil of sin or its cause, so they cannot shun its cause or hate it. Likewise, those who do not recognize good and the cause of good, that is, virtue, can neither love nor desire me, Goodness itself, or the virtue I have given you as a means and instrument for grace from me, the true Good.

So you see how much you need this light, for your sin consists simply in loving what I hate and hating what I love. I love virtue and I hate vice. So whoever loves vice and hates virtue offends me and loses my grace. Such people behave as if they were blind. Not recognizing the cause of vice, sensual selfishness, they have neither contempt for themselves nor knowledge of vice and the evil vice brings upon them. Nor do they know virtue or me, the Source of life-giving virtue, or the dignity they should preserve in themselves by coming to grace through virtue.

So you see, lack of knowledge is the cause of their evil. How necessary it is, then, for you to have this light!

99

But once the soul has gained this ordinary light she ought not rest content. For as long as you are pilgrims in this life you are capable of growing and should grow. Those who are not growing are by that very fact going backward. Either you should be growing in that ordinary light that you have gained with the help of my grace, or you should be making a genuine effort to advance to the second and more perfect light, to rise from the imperfect to the perfect. For the light gives the soul the will to advance to perfection.

In this second light there are two sorts of perfect souls. The perfect are those who have risen above the ordinary worldly way of living, and there are two sorts. The first are those who give themselves perfectly to punishing their bodies by performing severe and enormous penances. To keep their sensuality from rebelling against reason, these have all set their object more in mortifying their bodies than in slaying their selfish wills. They feed at the table of penance, and they are good and perfect if their penance has its root in me and is guided by the light of discernment. In other words, they must truly know themselves and me, be very humble, and be wholly subject to the judgments of my will rather than to those of other people.

But if they are not thus truly and humbly clothed in my will, they may often sin against their very perfection by setting themselves up as judges over those whose way is not the same as theirs. Do you know why this happens? Because they have invested more effort and desire in mortifying their bodies than in slaying their selfish wills. They are always wanting to choose times and places and spiritual consolations in their own way, and even earthly troubles and conflict with the devil (the way I told you about in the second, imperfect, stage). They are their very own deceivers, deceived by that selfish will that I have called "spiritual self-will," and in their self-delusion they say: "I would like to have this consolation rather than this conflict or trouble with the devil. Nor is it for myself that I say this, but to be more pleasing to God and to have more grace in my soul. For it seems to me I could serve and posses him better in this way than in that."

In this way they often fall into suffering and weariness, and so become insupportable to themselves and sin against their very perfection. And they are not even aware that they are lying there in the filth of their pride. But there they lie. For if it were not so, if they were truly humble and not presumptuous, they would see by the light that I, gentle first Truth, name the situation, the time, and the place, consolations or trials, whatever is necessary for salvation and to bring souls to the perfection for which I chose them. And they would see that everything I give is for love, and that therefore they should accept everything with love and reverence. This is what the others do, those who reach the third stage, as I shall tell you. These two sorts of people both live in this most perfect light.

100

Those who reach the third stage (which follows after the other) are perfect in every situation once they have come into this glorious light. No matter what I send them, they hold it in due reverence, as I mentioned when I spoke to you about the third and unitive stages of the soul. They consider themselves deserving of sufferings and outrages from the world, worthy to be deprived of any consolation at all that may be theirs. And just as they consider themselves deserving of suffering, so they also count themselves unworthy of any fruit that may come to them from their suffering. These have known and tasted in the light my eternal will, which wants only your good and permits you these things so that you may be made holy in me.

After the soul has come to know my will she clothes herself in it and attends only to how she may keep and intensify her perfection for the glory and praise of my name. In the light of faith she fixes her mind's eye on Christ crucified, my only-begotten Son, loving and following his teaching, which is rule and way for the perfect and imperfect alike. She sees how the Lamb my Truth is in love with her and instructs her in perfection, and seeing it, she falls in love with him. Perfection is what she came to know when she saw this gentle loving Word, my only-begotten Son, finding his nourishment at the table of holy desire by seeking honor for me his eternal Father and salvation for you. In this desire he ran eagerly to his shameful death on the cross and fulfilled the obedience that I his Father had laid on him. He did not shun toil or shame, did not hold back because of your ingratitude and foolish failure to recognize the great favor he had done you. The hounding of the Jews could not hold him back, nor the jeering insults and grumbling, nor the shouts of the people. He went through it all like a true knight and captain whom I had put on the battlefield to wrest you from the devil's hands. He freed you from the most perverse slavery there could be. This is why he instructed you in his way, his teaching, his rule. And this is why you can approach the gate to me, eternal Life, with the key of his precious blood that was poured out with such burning love, with hatred and contempt for your sins.

It is as if this gentle loving Word, my Son, were saying to you: "Look. I have made the road and opened the gate for you with my blood. Do not fail, then, to follow it. Do not sit down to rest out of selfish concern for yourself, foolishly saying you do not know the way. Do not presume to choose your own way of serving instead of the one I have made for you in my own person, eternal Truth, incarnate Word, the straight way hammered out with my own blood."

Get up, then, and follow him, for no one can come to me the Father except through him. He is the way and the gate through whom you must enter into me, the sea of peace.

When the soul, then, has come to taste this light after so delightfully seeing and knowing it, she runs to the table of holy desire, in love as she is and eager with a lover's restlessness. She has no eyes for herself, for seeking her own spiritual or material comfort. Rather, as one who has completely drowned her own will in this light and knowledge, she shuns no burden, from whatever source it may come. She even endures the pain of shame and vexations from the devil and other people's grumbling, feasting at the table of the most holy cross on honor for me, God eternal, and salvation for others.

She seeks no recompense either from me or from others, because she is stripped of any mercenary love, of any loving me for her own profit. She is clothed in perfect light, and loves me sincerely without any other concern than the glory and praise of my name. She does not serve me for her own pleasure or her neighbors for her own profit, but only for love.

Souls such as these have let go of themselves, have stripped off their old nature, their selfish sensuality, and clothed themselves in a new nature, the gentle Christ Jesus, my Truth, and they follow him courageously. These are they who have sat down at the table of holy desire, and have set their minds more on slaying their selfish will than on mortifying and killing their bodies. They have, it is true, mortified their bodies, but not as their chief concern. Rather, they have used mortification as the instrument it is to help them slay their self-will. (I told you this when I was explaining my statement that I would have few words and many deeds.) And this is what you should do. Your chief desire ought to be to slay your selfish will so that it neither seeks nor wants anything but to follow my gentle Truth, Christ crucified, by seeking the honor and glory of my name and the salvation of souls.

Those who live in this gentle light do just this. Therefore they are always peaceful and calm, and nothing can scandalize them because they have done away with what causes them to take scandal, their self-will. They trample underfoot all the persecutions the world and the devil can hound them with. They can stand in the water of great troubles and temptations, but it cannot hurt them because they are anchored to the vine of burning desire.

They find joy in everything. They do not sit in judgment on my servants or anyone else, but rejoice in every situation and every way of living they see, saying, "Thanks to you, eternal Father, that in your house there are so many dwelling places!" And they are happier to see many different ways than if they were to see everyone walking the same way, because this way they see the greatness of my goodness more fully revealed. In everything they find joy and the fragrance of the rose. This is true not only of good things; even when they see something that is clearly sinful they do not pass judgment, but rather feel a holy and genuine compassion, praying for the sinner and saying with perfect humility, "Today it is your turn; tomorrow it will be mine unless divine grace holds me up."

O dearest daughter, let the love of this sweet marvelous state take hold of you. Look at those who run along in this glorious light and their own magnificence. Their spirits are holy and they feast at the table of holy desire. By this light they have come to find their nourishment in the food of souls for the honor of me the eternal Father. They are clothed in the lovely garment, the teaching, of the Lamb, my only-begotten Son, with flaming charity.

They do not waste their time passing false judgment, either against my servants or the world's servants. They are not scandalized by any grumbling on anyone's part: if it is against themselves they are happy to suffer for my name, and when it is against someone else they bear with it in compassion for their neighbor, grumbling neither against the grumbler nor the victim, because their love for me and for their neighbor is well ordered. And because their love is well ordered, dearest daughter, they are never scandalized in those they love, nor in any person, because in this regard they are blind, and therefore they assume no right to be concerned with the intentions of other people but only with discerning my merciful will.

They are faithful to the teaching that you know my Truth gave you early in your life when you asked with great longing to be led to perfect purity. You know that when you were wondering how you might attain this, your desire was answered while you were asleep. The voice sounded not only in your mind but in your ear as well—so much so, if you recall, that you returned to your bodily senses when my Truth spoke thus to you:

"Do you wish to reach perfect purity and be so freed from scandal that your spirit will not take scandal in anything at all? Then see that you remain united with me in loving affection, for I am supreme and eternal purity. I am the fire that purifies the soul. So the nearer the soul comes to me the more pure she will become, and the more she departs from me the more unclean she is. This is why worldly folk fall into such wickedness, because they have left me. But the soul who unites herself directly with me shares in my own purity.

"There is another thing you must do to attain this union and purity: You must never pass judgment in human terms on anything you see or hear from anyone at all, whether it concerns you or someone else. You must consider only my will for them and for you.

"And if you should see something that is clearly a sin or fault, snatch the rose from that thorn. In other words, offer these things to me in holy compassion. As for any assault against yourself, consider that my will permits it to prove virtue in you and in my other servants. And assume that the offender does such a thing as an instrument commissioned by me. For often such a person's intention is good; there is no one who can judge the hidden heart.

"When you cannot see clearly and openly whether the sin is deadly, you must not pass judgment in your mind, but be concerned only about my will for that person. And if you do see it, you must respond not with judgment but with holy compassion. In this way you will attain perfect purity, for if you act this way your spirit will not be scandalized either in me or in your neighbors. For you cast contempt on your neighbors when you pay attention to their ill will toward you rather than my will for them. Such contempt and scandal alienates the soul from me, blocks her perfection, and to some extent deprives her of grace—in proportion to the seriousness of the contempt and hatred she has conceived for her neighbor because of her judgmental thoughts.

"Things go just the opposite for the soul who is concerned for my will. For I will only your well-being, and whatever I give, I give it so that you may reach the goal for which I created you. The soul who considers things in this light remains always in love for her neighbors, and so she remains in my love. And because she remains in my love she remains united with me.

"So if you would attain the purity you ask of me, there are three principal things you must do. You must be united with me in loving affection, bearing in your memory the blessings you have received from me. With the eye of your understanding you must see my affectionate charity, how unspeakably much I love you. And where the human will is concerned you must consider my will rather than people's evil intentions, for I am their judge— not you, but I. If you do this, all perfection will be yours."

This, if you remember well, was the teaching my Truth gave you.

Now I tell you, dearest daughter, those who have learned this teaching taste the pledge of eternal life even in this life. If you keep this teaching in mind you will fall neither into the devil's trap (for you will recognize it) nor into the traps you asked me about.

Antoninus Fierozzi (1389–1459) and
John of Fiesole (Fra Angelico) (c. 1400–1455)

Antoninus Fierozzi was born in Florence, Italy, in 1389 and joined the Order of Friars Preachers in 1405 under the guidance of John Dominici, one of the leaders of the Dominican reform movement initiated by Catherine of Siena and her confessor Raymond of Capua. Antoninus became one of the founding members of the reformed priory at Fiesole, not far from Florence, in 1406. After completing his studies for the priesthood, Antoninus was asked to serve as prior at Cortona. In 1421 Antoninus was called back to Fiesole as prior, and it was there in 1422 that he would receive the young artist John of Fiesole, later to be known as Fra Angelico, into the Dominican Order.

Fra Angelico was born around 1400 in Tuscany, Italy, and worked in Florence as a painter before entering the novitiate of the reformed Dominicans. The period of Fra Angelico's religious formation under Antoninus from 1421 to 1426 provided the opportunity for the prior of Fiesole to share with the young artist the vision of Dominican life that he himself had received from John Dominici. The bonds between Antoninus and Fra Angelico and the common vision of a renewed Dominican life that they shared continued to develop as their lives unfolded together during the next thirty years. Each complemented the other, and together these two holy friars left a breathtaking legacy of art and spirituality.

In 1432 Antoninus was appointed vicar-general for the reformed Dominicans of Tuscany. Under the patronage of Cosimo de Medici the former Benedictine monastery of San Marco in Florence was given to the reformed Dominicans in 1436. The rebuilding of San Marco as a center for Dominican life and mission began the following year. With the election of Antoninus as prior in 1439, the work of restoration took on new momentum. As vicar of the Roman/Tuscan reformed Dominicans from

1437 to 1446 and as prior of San Marco from 1439 to 1444, Antoninus was responsible for the creation of a center of Dominican life and spirituality that would sustain the contemplative life of the reformed friars and give them the vision and courage necessary for the mission of preaching. As a Florentine himself, Antoninus was profoundly aware of the needs of the laity of this great Renaissance city to hear the Gospel and to experience renewal in their own Christian vocations.

During the formative years of the San Marco community Fra Angelico was vicar at Fiesole and thus shared with Antoninus the responsibility for maintaining the ideals of the reformed Dominicans of Florence and Fiesole. Out of their sense of shared responsibility for the future of the reform movement, Antoninus and Fra Angelico came to see the possibility of creating something strikingly new at San Marco.

Between 1440 and 1454 Antoninus was in the midst of writing his *Summa Moralis*, a systematic and comprehensive presentation of all the aspects of Christian moral theology. It was intended to serve in forming and guiding the preaching and confessional ministries of his Dominican brothers. While he was writing, Antoninus began to realize that Fra Angelico could do by painting in the realm of spiritual theology what he was doing by words in the realm of moral theology, that is, create a *summa,* an ordered presentation of essential truths. By his painting, Fra Angelico would transform the walls of the priory of San Marco into a visible *summa* of Dominican spirituality.

San Marco, however, was not only to be a pictorial *summa* of Dominican spirituality as envisioned by the reform movement, but also a *summa* of Christian life, patterned after Antoninus' *Summa Moralis*, for the members of the Florentine lay confraternities that met at San Marco under the leadership of Cosimo de Medici. For Antoninus and Fra Angelico the Dominican ministry of contemplative preaching in Florence was the proclamation in word and image of the essentials of the Christian faith to a society profoundly influenced by the ideals of Renaissance humanism. The essential elements within the vision of Christian humanism formulated by Antoninus would be visually formulated in an iconographic program that appealed to and transformed the deepest ideals of Renaissance society. The themes central to the Dominican reform movement in the writings of Catherine of Siena and John Dominici and the vision of Christian humanism presented verbally in Antoninus' *Summa Moralis* would take flesh visually in the common rooms, the corridors, the friars' cells, and the lay guests' cells at San Marco. Through the common vision and ministry of Antoninus and Fra Angelico, San Marco became a Dominican center of life and hope where the Gospel would be preached through the beauty of art.

Antoninus was made Archbishop of Florence by Pope Eugene IV in 1446 and served as a model pastor until his death in 1459. He was canonized in 1523 by Pope Hadrian VI. Fra Angelico was in Rome from 1446 until 1449 painting four fresco cycles at the Vatican. He returned to Fiesole in 1450 to become prior at San Domenico. He died in 1455 and was beatified by Pope John Paul II in 1982. The selections that follow are from Antoninus' *Summa Moralis* and from an address by Pope Pius XII at the opening of an exhibition of the paintings of Fra Angelico at the Vatican in 1955.

Thomas C. McGonigle, o.p.

From the Prologue of *Summa Moralis*

> *"The world teaches us wisdom, not only about*
> *divine matters, but also about what we are to do."*

How great are your works, O Lord! In wisdom you have made them all. The earth is full of your creatures. In the joy of his heart the prophet contemplates the divine majesty and is overcome by the extent of divine goodness manifested in the works of God. And so he exclaims: *How great are your works!* He seems to show the mystery of the most holy Trinity, that Trinity to whom we should always appeal and whose help we should always await. In this way our good works which spring from the Trinity may be brought to their fulfillment. As Plato says, without this greatest of beings no nature would subsist, there would be no understanding, and no action would come to its term. And should one forget this being, nothing could be truly undertaken.

Consequently, in the first phrase of this passage the prophet suggests that remarkable power which is attributed to the Father: *How great are your works, O Lord!* In the second phrase he speaks of the extraordinary wisdom that is attributed to the Son: *In wisdom you have made them all.* Finally he mentions the immeasurable kindness that is attributed to the Spirit: *The earth is full of your creatures.*

In addressing God Mordechai speaks of that remarkable power which is shown forth in creation: *O Lord, almighty king, all things are in your power . . . You have made heaven and earth and every wonderful thing under the heavens.* Here he shows that by this greatest of all powers, which is attributed to the Father, all things were made from nothing, unlike the things made by an artisan which require some kind of material.

As far as wisdom is concerned, Sirach says: *The source of wisdom is the Word of God in heaven. All things came to be through him.* The Word, the Son of God, is as it were the skill of the almighty Father in whom and by whom all things have been made very good. *In wisdom you have made them all.* And since it pertains to the wise to put things in order, it is because of him that everything is harmoniously arranged; it is because of him that the universe is beautiful and that divine providence governs the world. *In wisdom you have made them all.*

The world is a book, written both within and without, which instructs us about wisdom. It instructs us about the wisdom of the divine mystery, as the letter to the Romans says: *Since the creation of the world the invisible attributes of eternal power can be perceived in what God has made.* It also instructs us about wisdom in action, as we can read in the book of Job: *Ask the beasts to teach you, and the birds of the air to tell you; or the reptiles on earth to instruct you, and the fish of the sea to inform you.* For everyone can perceive how God provides for creation. God never abandons it, continues to communicate with it, makes the earth and trees fruitful, is never idle, and offers countless testimonies to us concerning the qualities necessary for living well. And so *in wisdom you have made them all* to give us wisdom.

Concerning the immeasurable kindness of God, Saint Augustine tells us that this is clearly evident from all that God does for us, all done with great power and wisdom. And so the prophet adds: *The earth is full of your creatures.* We are the earth, we come from the earth, we return to the earth, we cultivate the earth, and we live from the earth. And this earth is filled with God's creatures.

God possesses all that is of earth, all that is of heaven and all that is divine. With all of this God *fills the earth,* that is, the human race. For God gives us the things of earth for our use: *You have put all things under our feet.* God gives us the things of heaven, that is, the angels, as servants: *Are they not all ministering spirits sent to serve?* What greater possession does God have than the Son! We were filled up with God, when *the Word became flesh. God so loved the world,* that is, "us," *that he gave his only Son.* And so one can clearly say: The earth is full of your creatures.

***

From an address of Pope Pius XII at the opening of an exhibition of paintings of Fra Angelico at the Vatican (April 20, 1955)

"Whoever does the work of Christ should always remain with Christ."

Today after five centuries we gladly honor this holy friar and consummate artist, giving further import to his well-deserved tribute. The humble and pious Blessed John of Fiesole came to this Apostolic Palace at the peak of his artistic maturity at the request of our predecessors, first of Eugene IV, and later of the great patron of the arts Nicholas V. Here on these walls Fra Angelico immortalized some of the most vivid creations of his artistic imagination, an honor and adornment of the Apostolic residence and a perennial witness of the perfect accord between religion and art.

Freed from the popular and pious legend which depicted the fervent friar painting his saints while absorbed in unconscious ecstasy, his brush guided by supraterrestrial beings, his individuality has now been set in its true light. This does not mean, however, that his profound religious sense, his serene and austere asceticism nourished by solid virtue, contemplation and prayer, did not exercise a determining influence on his artistic expression. Rather it provided the power and immediacy with which his art spoke to the minds of others and, as has frequently been noted, transformed it into prayer. For he was in the habit of repeating "whoever does the work of Christ should always remain with Christ."

The genuine piety of Fra Angelico is rightly considered an essential basis for his success as a painter. Still another basis can be discovered in his cultural formation, that is, in the universal doctrine he learned in the school of the "perrenial philosophy" and to which he adhered with clear and tranquil certitude. Many critics have rightly pointed out how Thomistic doctrine is reflected not only in the content of his paintings but also in his style and technique.

Certainly Fra Angelico's painting is always religious, both in subject matter and in style and method of treatment. Accustomed to the tranquility of monastic discipline and striving always for perfection in intention, in word, and in action, it is natural he should seek to attain it also in the techniques of his art, which as a result is always cleanly bright and serene. In his life, as in his paintings, there are no moments of exterior drama, but inner struggles, fought in complete resignation to the divine will and with calm confidence in the victory of good. The very light which pours over his figures and through his backgrounds is measurable not so much by its intensity as by its purity; it is, in so far as possible, a celestial light.

His themes are simple and linear, patterned as it were on the style of the evangelists. His figures always reveal an intense interior life. Their countenances, their gestures, and their movements are all transfigured by it. As he narrates or expounds the divine mysteries to his audience, Fra Angelico is ever the skillfull "preacher," seeking to elicit an immediate response with descriptive and decorative elements in order to speak more quietly to the inmost soul.

On one hand his purpose is to teach the truths of faith, convincing human minds by the very force of their beauty. On the other he aims to lead the faithful to the practice of Christian virtues by setting before them beautiful and attractive examples. This second purpose renders his work a perennial message of living Christianity and, in a certain sense, a sublimely human message based on the principle of the transhumanizing force of religion. It is by the power of religion that everyone who comes in direct contact with God and the divine mysteries becomes like God in holiness, in beauty and in blessedness. They become, that is, creatures fashioned according to the original design of their Creator. Fra Angelico's brush, therefore, gives life to a kind of model human being, not unlike the angels, in whom all is balanced, serene, perfect: a model Christian, rarely found perhaps in the circumstances of earthly life, but still to be offered for imitation by the people.

Bartolomé de Las Casas (1484–1566)

Bartolomé de Las Casas was born in Seville, Spain in 1484. His father, Pedro, was a merchant who accompanied Christopher Columbus on his second voyage to the New World in 1493. When Pedro returned to Spain in 1498, fourteen-year-old Bartolomé announced to his father that he wished to begin studies for the priesthood. After four years at the University of Salamanca, Bartolomé decided to interrupt his studies and join his father, who had returned to the New World. Father and son worked together running a plantation on the island of Hispaniola and acting as provisioners for other colonists and the Spanish military authorities.

The violent treatment of the Indians during these early days of Spanish conquest made a profound impression on Las Casas. In 1506 he went back to Spain and resumed his studies for the priesthood. He was ordained in Rome in 1507 and returned to Hispaniola in 1510 with the new governor of the Antilles, Bartholomew Columbus, Christopher's elder brother. Las Casas was engaged in his ministry as an Indian catechist when the Dominicans under the leadership of Fray Pedro de Cordoba arrived to begin their preaching ministry in the New World. In December of 1511 the firm commitment of the Friars Preachers to defend the rights of the Indians was expressed through the preaching of Fray Anton Montesino in the Cathedral of Santo Domingo. He said that those who continued to oppress the Indians through the cruel treatment and exploitation of the *encomienda* were committing mortal sin. The *encomienda* was a system that allowed the Spaniards to collect tribute from the Indians and use them as laborers. In return the new Spanish landholders were supposed to protect the Indians, provide for their needs, and see that they were instructed in the Christian faith. In many instances the colonists ignored their responsibilities and treated the native population with great injustice and brutality.

The preaching of the Dominicans brought Las Casas to the realization that he had not done enough in his own ministry to oppose the exploitation and decimation of the Indians. In 1514 a conversion experience led him to the conviction that he was to join with the Dominicans in doing everything possible to secure the rights of the Indians to their land and their freedom. Las Casas and Montesino set sail for Spain in 1515 to place their appeals for just treatment of the Indians before King Ferdinand. They knew that they were facing formidable opposition to any changes in the *encomienda,* both from the royal court and from the Spanish settlers.

When Las Casas and Montesino arrived in Spain, King Ferdinand was seriously ill and would die shortly after an initial interview. Las Casas then approached Cardinal Cisneros, aging regent for the new King, Charles I of Spain, who would also become Charles V, Holy Roman Emperor, in 1519. Although he received some moral and financial support from Cisneros and King Charles from 1515 to 1522, Las Casas' plan for agricultural communities in the New World, where peasants from Castile and Indians would work side by side as equals, failed due to ongoing opposition to his work on both sides of the Atlantic as well as Indian revolts in 1522.

Las Casas' response to this failure in his attempt to protect and serve the Indians was to make a new beginning in 1522, at the age of thirty-eight, by joining the Order of Preachers. The Dominican vision of study as the constant support for preaching opened new horizons for Las Casas as he read Aristotle, the *Summa theologica* of St. Thomas Aquinas, and the recently completed *Commentary* on the *Summa* by Thomas de Vio Cajetan, the great Dominican theologian and cardinal. Writing as preaching, flowing from study and prayer, became a new way for Las Casas to seek justice for the Indians. His masterpiece in 1534 would be *The Only Way to Draw All People to a Living Faith.* Las Casas tried to show that the war, brutality, forced labor, and oppression that had accompanied the Spanish conquest of the New World needed to be replaced by a peaceful proclamation of the Gospel that respected the human dignity and rights of the Indians. Assisted by his Dominican brothers in the New World and Spain, Las Casas received the support of Rome for his vision of evangelization through the papal bull *Sublimis Deus* in 1537. He also received help from the Emperor Charles V in 1542 through the publication of the *New Laws* that sought to protect the freedom and rights of the Indians.

A new stage of life and ministry began for Las Casas in 1543 when he was named Bishop of Chiapas in Mexico. The four years of Las Casas' active ministry as a bishop taught him that laws promulgated in Spain were of no use in protecting the Indians unless they were actually enforced in the New World. In 1547 he resigned from his diocese and returned to Spain so that he could be an advocate and voice of conscience at the royal court and help to oversee promulgation and implementation of laws that affected the rights of the Indians.

At the end of his life Las Casas, who had spent his life seeking justice for others, deeply regretted that while he was opposed to the slave trade, he had supported the limited importation of black slaves as a way of relieving the suffering of the Indians. He died in Madrid at the age of eighty-two in 1566, grateful to God that he had kept faith for fifty years, pleading for the restoration to the Indians of their original lands, liberty, and freedom. The legacy of Las Casas is his witness through his life and writings, especially *The Only Way*, to the Gospel that proclaims the dignity and value of every human being and the responsibility peacefully to seek justice and freedom for all.

The selections that follow are taken from *The Only Way*.

Thomas C. McGonigle, o.p.

From *The Only Way*

The Ideal Missionary

We can select out five basic traits that reveal as a whole how the gospel must be preached according to the mind and mandate of Christ.

One. Those who hear the gospel preached, non-Christians especially, must sense that the preachers want no power over them as a result of the preaching. Chrysostom's view. He said that when Paul preached, Paul did not use the language of seduction nor the language of deceit. The seducer wants power, the politician wants control. "No one can say we lied to gain control of people." It comes down to Paul's statement: "We are not after glory from human beings; not from you, not from anyone else" (1 Thessalonians 2:6). Paul's success had provoked suspicion. Chrysostom thinks he said what he said to get rid of that suspicion.

Two. Those who hear the gospel preached, non-Christians especially, must sense that the preachers are not really itching after their wealth. So Paul says: "Preaching cannot be a cover for greed" (1 Thessalonians 2:5). Or, in Anselm's wording: We were not after what you had when we preached, it was not our wish; we kept to the Lord's instruction, the one which went to the root of all evil. He forbade the apostles to keep gold or silver or any coin. St. Jerome, reflecting on Matthew's Gospel, says that if the apostles made money, people would think they preached for lucre's sake, not for the sake of saving souls. Whatever they then said would be laughed at as propaganda. Chrysostom says, about this second rule: (1) The precept of poverty frees the disciples from suspicion. (2) It frees them from worldly worry—their entire concern can be for the word of God. Paul states the matter: "It was trust in God that let us preach the Gospel to you without stint" (1 Thessalonians 2:2). (3) He showed them that He, Christ, was their power. Christ's question later brought it home: "What else did you need that time you preached?" (Luke 22:35).

Three. Preachers should address audiences, especially non-Christian, with modesty and respect. They should create a climate of kindness and calm and graciousness so that their hearers would want to listen and would have a greater respect for the message. This is why Paul said: "I became like a child." Or a peaceful person, as I noted from Chrysostom: "I said nothing that smacked of arrogance" (Homily on 2 Thessalonians). And Chrysostom adds the words "in your midst," meaning "not wanting to lord it over any of you."

Four. There is a further trait to be drawn about what is crucially needed in the way one presents the faith, if the preacher is to save himself as well. It is the love called charity. Paul sought to save the whole world with it. Gentleness and patience and kindness are kindred spirits to charity. "Love is patient, it is kind, it suffers all things, it bears all things . . ." (1 Corinthians 13:4, 7). If you want proof of how his heart was on fire with charity, listen to him say: "So being affectionately desirous of you, we were willing to have imparted to you, not the Gospel of God only, but also our own souls, because you were dear to us" (1 Thessalonians 2:8). "Greater love than this no one has than that he lay down his life for his friends" (John 15:13). And notice what he said to the Corinthians. It shows how kind, how respectful his preaching was even to his persecutors, even to those who refused the faith a hearing. "I am afraid that God will make it humiliating for me when I come to visit you. I will be a reproach to those many who used to sin but have done no penance since for their former impurity and fornication and lewdness" (2 Corinthians 12:21). And: "My little ones, I am in constant labor until Christ is born in you" (Galatians 4:19). There was a lustful man whose lust grieved deeply. Paul grieved for the man more than the man for himself. He prayed for him: "Love this man even more" (2 Corinthians 2:8). And when Paul was absent from the community of the Church he lived a sad and lonely life: "For I wrote you out of much affliction and anguish of heart and with many tears, not to cause you pain but to let you know the abundant love that I have for you" (2 Corinthians 2:4). "To the Jews I became as a Jew, in order to win Jews; to those under the law I became as one under the law; to the weak, I became weak. I am made all things to all people so that I might save all" (1 Corinthians 9:20–22).

Five. It is found expressed already in Paul's words cited above. "You witnessed, as did God, the way I related to you who came to believe, how respectfully, how carefully, how honestly, how blamelessly" (1 Thessalonians 2:10). Words added to the text say: "both before and after your conversion."

"How respectfully," i.e., under God, as the gloss in the text notes, and St. Athanasius says also, doing all that has to be done with due reverence for God. And Anselm interprets it: "How respectfully . . . I related to you through the openness of all my dealings." "How carefully," is interpreted by the gloss on the text and Athanasius to mean, "doing right by my brethren, not wronging them, i.e., putting the squeeze on no one for their money." "How blamelessly," meaning a harm to no one.

Or, as Anselm reads it, "How carefully" keeping the balance of justice toward neighbors by doing right; and "How blamelessly, how straightforwardly and honestly I treated you, not to give you cause for complaint against me." Or, "How blameless I was toward you. I never criticized you when I had to live with your shortcomings. There was a reason to act this way toward you, to help you: something you all recognize, you know this, and something in addition, that it was with love I brought each of you around. . . ."

***

Clearly, the fifth element prescribed for the preaching of Christ's gospel is living example: a life visibly virtuous, a life that harms no one, a life blameless from any quarter. A teacher must live his own words, must teach by practice more than by presentation. A teacher who talks, only talks, has a frigid effect; in fact is not a teacher but a faker and two-faced. So apostles teach first by deeds, second by words. No need for words when their deeds did the preaching. The evidence shows they led such holy lives that those who carped at them carped at their doctrine not their decency. As Chrysostom puts it: "They put up with being called seducers and quacks for the Gospel's sake, but no one could ever scoff at their lives." No one ever called an apostle guilty of lust or greed, the accusation "seducers" described only their doctrine.

[Chrysostom continues:]

> You must respect someone whose moral life is a beacon, whose truth stops the critique even of enemies. It is not right to attack such people with curses and slander, the ones who live faultless lives—you can hear Christ saying as much: "So let your light shine before people that, seeing what you do, they may give glory to God the Father who is in heaven" (Matthew 5:16). No one but a blind man would call the sun black; what everyone else sees would shame his contention. The same concerning a man of great dignity, of great moral life, no one but a blind man would dare blame him. It's rather to attack the teachings that non-believers loose their barbs. They dare not loose them at the purity of his life. The life, they hold in awe and admiration, as does everyone.

Catherine de' Ricci (1522–1590)

Alessandra Lucrezia Romola de' Ricci was born in Florence, Italy on April 23, 1522, to Pierfrancesco de' Ricci and Catherine de' Panzano, of the Florentine Ricasoli family. Each of Catherine's parents brought noble lineage to her life. When Catherine—or Sandrina, as she was known as a child—was four, her mother died. Her father sent her to the nearby Benedictine monastery of San Pietro at Monticelli where two of Catherine's aunts were members of the community. Within two months of Catherine's mother's death her father married Fiamette da Diacceto, and eventually Catherine had four half-brothers and five half-sisters.

When she was barely nine, Catherine was scandalized by a bitter disagreement between two nuns at San Pietro over possession of a book, and she quickly left the monastery. Catherine probably went home to live among her stepmother's children, but even contemporary hagiographies report her longing to live a contemplative life. The modern mind does not easily accept the fact that Catherine determined her own vocation at the age of eleven when, in 1533, she met two nuns from the Dominican convent of San Vincenzo, founded at Prato in Tuscany in 1503 by nine women who were followers of the Dominican Friar Girolamo Savonarola. Catherine's uncle, the Dominican Friar Timoteo de' Ricci, was confessor to the convent. While the women at San Vincenzo were Third, not Second Order women, they lived enclosed. Her father objected, but Catherine finally entered the monastery and received the habit and her religious name—Catherine—in 1535.

Catherine proved to be a different sort of novice. Quite often she was found to be "sleepy," as she put it; we do not know if Catherine understood her ecstasies at first. It is certain her novice mistress and the other nuns did not. Catherine prayed, sometimes through the night, before a crucifix she brought from home. Her days—particularly Thursdays and Fridays—were passed as if in a trance. She made no good impression on the rest of the monastery, but despite their misgivings she was admitted to vows on May 24, 1536. She had just turned fifteen.

Catherine's raptures—the Italian word is "Ratti"—both distanced her from her contemporaries and joined her to their suffering. She credited Savonarola for her miraculous healing in 1540; she said he cured her with the sign of the cross, but only after she affirmed she wanted to be healed only if it was God's will, and with the admonition she not leave her cell until the infirmarian permitted it.

Catherine continued to suffer the derision of members of the convent and increasingly of others who heard about her ecstasies, which lasted precisely twenty-eight hours, beginning at noon on Thursdays, during which she acted and reacted to approximately seventeen "scenes" in the Passion of Christ, and after which she showed the wounds of stigmata. Her first "Ecstasy of the Passion" came to her in February 1542, and recurred weekly for twelve years, during which time she was subject to countless examinations and interviews, including and especially by the ever-changing Dominincan priors of nearby San Domenico, who technically were responsible for the convent. Given the times—the Inquisition was strong in Italy—there was serious danger of Catherine being branded a heretic. Each examination, including one conducted at the express command of Pope Paul III, sought to determine whether she was indeed possessed by the devil.

Even so, as her weekly reliving of the Passion continued, persons of every rank and status sought her out, including three future Popes: Cardinals Cervini (Pope Marcellus II), Alexander de Medici (Leo XI), and Aldobrandini (Clement VIII). After twelve years, at her request, the physical evidence of her reliving the Passion disappeared.

There is little original writing by Catherine near the time of her internalizing a theology of the cross, but her few early letters repeat the basic words of Christian life: humility, obedience, love, patience. Eventually Catherine's suffering with Christ opened the eyes of some who had doubted her. Despite the external attention and internal distrust of Catherine's ecstasies, the convent's founding prioress and former novice mistress asked Catherine to be sub-prioress. She also asked Catherine to provide a *summa* of the spiritual life. Catherine's sophisticated reply presents three stages, each with two steps that correspond to the triple development of love and culminate in the denial of self-will, the perfection of love. In the ordinary course of events, but with obvious reluctance—even tears—Catherine became prioress of a convent of one hundred nuns when she was barely thirty. Shortly thereafter, in the winter of 1552, her beloved uncle, Fra Timoteo de' Ricci, died at Perugia. For two decades Timoteo had helped keep the founding spirit—the reforms of Savonarola—alive in San Vincenzo.

It is from this period of Catherine's life that we have the most abundant evidence of her writing, through the day-to-day affairs of running the monastery. There are letters to her sisters and to the Friars, letters to rulers and prelates. She was affirmed to have had the power of bilocation by Philip Neri, who with five others saw her present in Rome while she was known to be in Tuscany. She corresponded with the Carmelite nun and stigmatist Mary Magdalene de' Pazzi (1566–1607) and with Alessandro Luzzago. In addition, a few of Catherine's letters to her disciples survive.

Catherine died at the age of 68 on February 2, 1690, and she was buried at the convent of San Vicenzio, which has come to be known as Santa Caterina, in Prato. Her canonization process was much delayed, as the reports of her life and connection to Savonarola were examined and reexamined. Catherine was beatified in 1732 by Clement XII, and canonized in 1746 by Benedict XIV. Her feast is celebrated on February 13, and she takes under her patronage those who suffer illness.

The letter below is assumed to be her letter to Maria Maddelena Strozzi.

Phyllis Zagano

From *A Letter to a Nun, November 18, 1549*

"Very dear daughter,—I have already sent you a letter to exhort you to the service of our Lord; and now I send you this one, in which I am going to give—first for myself, and then for you—an account of the true way of faithfully serving our Divine Spouse, and a *résumé* of the spiritual life; so that, by following it, we shall carry out the holy will of God. If, then, my daughter, you would be the true spouse of Jesus, you must do His holy will in all things; and you will do this if you entirely give up your own will on every occasion, and if you love the divine Spouse with your whole heart, your whole soul, and your whole strength. Then, you must carefully attend to the following points (but it is necessary to weigh all these words), as they contain the summary of Christian perfection:

"1. We must force ourselves to detach the heart and the will from all earthly love; to love no fleeting things, except for the love of God; and, above all, not to love God for our own sakes for self-interest, but with a love as pure as His own goodness.

"2. We must direct all our thoughts, words and actions to His honour; and by prayer, counsel, and good example seek His glory solely, whether for ourselves or for others, so that through our means all may love and honour God. This second thing is more pleasing to Him than the first, as it better fulfils His will.

"3. We must aim more and more at the accomplishment of the divine will: not only desiring nothing special to happen to us, bad or even good, in this wretched life, and thus keeping ourselves always at God's disposal, with heart and soul at peace; but also believing with a firm faith that Almighty God loves us more than we love ourselves, and takes more care of us than we could take of ourselves.

"The more we conform to this way of acting, the more we shall find God present to help us, and the more we shall experience His most gentle love. But no one can reach such perfection except by constant and courageous sacrifice of self-will; and, if we would learn to practice such abnegation, it is necessary to keep ourselves in a state of great and deep humility, so that by perfect knowledge of our own misery and weakness we may rise to learn the greatness and beauty of our God. Consider how just and necessary it is to serve Him unceasingly, with love and obedience. I say just, because God being Father and Master of all things, it is just that His son and servant should obey and love Him: I say necessary, because by acting otherwise we could not be saved. Let us always remember, never doubting, that it is the eternal, sovereign, all-powerful God who does, orders, or allows everything that happens, and that nothing comes to pass without His divine will. Let us remember that He is Himself that wisdom which, in the government of the universe—of heaven, earth, and every single creature—cannot be deceived (He would be neither God nor most wise, if it were otherwise). Let us look upon Him as supremely good, loving and beneficent. If, through His mercy, this conviction becomes strongly impressed upon our wills, we shall easily take all things from His sacred hand with well-contented hearts, always thanking Him for fulfilling His most holy will in us; because, by acting thus (with the help of His holy grace) we shall unite ourselves to Him by true love in this life and by glory in eternity. May

He grant it to us in His goodness! Of your charity pray for me, a wretched sinner, who commends herself to you all.

Your sister in Christ.

Martin de Porres (1579–1639)

Martin de Porres was born in Lima, Peru in 1579. His father, Don Juan de Porres, was a Spanish hidalgo and his mother, Aña Velazquez, was a freed black slave from Panama. Although Don Juan initially refused to recognize either Martin or his younger sister as his children, thus rendering them illegitimate, he did not entirely abandon his paternal responsibilities. Realizing the giftedness of his children, he eventually took both of them with him to Ecuador, where he recognized them as his legitimate offspring and provided them with some education. When Don Juan was appointed governor of Panama in 1587 he sent Martin and his sister back to their mother in Lima. However, Don Juan did have his son apprenticed to a barber-surgeon, which meant that Martin would acquire skills, especially knowledge of medicine, to support himself in the future.

In Lima the young Martin de Porres found himself face to face with the complex realities of Spain's colonial empire in the New World. In 1530 Francisco Pizarro with about one hundred eighty men had landed on the Pacific coast of South America to begin the conquest of the vast Inca empire. By 1535 he had been successful in his efforts and established his capital for this new territory of Spain's empire at Lima. The Peruvian city grew quickly and soon contained a diverse population of conquering Spaniards from different social classes, conquered Incas, black slaves imported from Africa, and mulattoes like Martin, who belonged racially to two worlds but would often be seen as an outsider by both groups.

Martin de Porres, however, chose to see his life situation as the son of a Spanish hidalgo and a freed black slave not as a disadvantage but rather as a call from God to walk in holiness through a life of humble service to all who lived in Lima. In 1590, at the age of fifteen, Martin came to the Dominican Priory of Santo Domingo, also called Santo Rosario, and asked to be received as a tertiary, a member of the Third Order, who would serve the needs of the community as a *donado*, receiving food and housing in return for his labors. Martin's father and Juan de Lorenzana, the Dominican prior, encouraged the young man to enter as a lay brother, a full member of the First Order, rather than a tertiary. Martin, however, chose to live the humble role of a *donado* for eight years before entering and being solemnly professed in the First Order as a lay or cooperator brother in 1603.

Pizarro had given the Dominicans, who accompanied him, the land on which they began building the Priory of Santo Domingo in 1540. The members of the large Dominican community who were living there when Martin entered the Order were engaged in diverse ministries of preaching and pastoral care in the city including teaching at the University of San Marcos, established in 1551. Martin was involved both in internal ministry to the Dominican community as barber, surgeon, wardrobe-keeper, and infirmarian, and in external ministry to the poor and sick of the city.

Martin's humble service to the poor and all in need was a profound expression of his vow of poverty as a Dominican and his commitment to preach the Gospel by living the pattern of Jesus' ministry to all, especially the outsiders in society. In a world that was very conscious of social class and race, he was sometimes subjected to humiliations because he was a mulatto and a lay brother. Martin's response from his life of prayer and penance was always forgiveness and a constant outreach of mercy that brought physical and spiritual healing and strength to whoever needed support and comfort.

Seventeenth-century Lima witnessed the holiness not only of Martin de Porres, but also of two of his Dominican friends, St. Rose of Lima (1586–1617), a Dominican tertiary, and St. Juan Macias, a lay brother at the Dominican Priory of St. Mary Magdalene (1585–1645). Each of the three saints witnessed in a unique way to service of the poor and lives of prayer and penance, interceding for God's mercy on the complex society of the capital of Spain's colonial empire in South America. When Martin de Porres died at the age of sixty in 1639, people from all walks of life and all classes of society came to honor the humble mulatto Dominican brother who had sought to serve them unreservedly in their spiritual and temporal needs. Martin de Porres was beatified in 1837 and canonized by Pope John XXIII in 1962. He is the patron of social justice and race relations.

Martin wrote nothing. In fact, it is not known if he even knew how to write. The selections that follow are taken from the canonization homily of Pope John XXIII.

Thomas C. McGonigle, O.P.

From a homily at the Canonization of Saint Martin de Porres by Pope John XXIII

"Martin the Charitable"

The example of Martin's life is ample evidence that we can strive for holiness and salvation as Christ Jesus has shown us: first, by loving God *with all your heart, with all your soul, and with all your mind*; and second, *by loving your neighbor as yourself.*

When Martin had come to realize that Christ Jesus *suffered for us and that he carried our sins on his body to the cross,* he would meditate with remarkable ardor and affection about Christ on the cross. Whenever he would contemplate Christ's terrible torture he would be reduced to tears. He had an exceptional love for the great sacrament of the eucharist and often spent long hours in prayer before the blessed sacrament. His desire was to receive the sacrament in communion as often as he could.

Saint Martin, always obedient and inspired by his divine teacher, dealt with his brothers with that profound love which comes from pure faith and humility of spirit. He loved men because he honestly looked on them as God's children and as his own brothers and sisters. Such was his humility that he loved them even more than himself and considered them to be better and more righteous than he was.

He did not blame others for their shortcomings. Certain that he deserved more severe punishment for his sins than others did, he would overlook their worst offenses. He was tireless in his efforts to reform the criminal, and he would sit up with the sick to bring them comfort. For the poor he would provide food, clothing and medicine. He did all he could to care for poor farmhands, blacks and mulattoes who were looked down upon as slaves, the dregs of society in their time. Common people responded by calling him "Martin the charitable."

The virtuous example and even the conversation of this saintly man exerted a powerful influence in drawing men to religion. It is remarkable how even today his influence can still move us toward the things of heaven. Sad to say, not all of us understand these spiritual values as well as we should, nor do we give them a proper place in our lives. Many of us, in fact, strongly attracted by sin, may look upon these values as of little moment, even something of a nuisance, or we ignore them altogether. It is deeply rewarding for men striving for salvation to follow in Christ's footsteps and to obey God's commandments. If only everyone could learn this lesson from the example that Martin gave us.

Henri Dominique Lacordaire (1802–1861)

Henri Dominique Lacordaire was born in Recey-sur-Ource in Burgundy, France in 1802. Lacordaire's father was a surgeon and his mother came from a family of lawyers. The world into which Lacordaire was born was ruled by Napoléon Bonaparte, who was using the ideals of the French Revolution to build an empire that would redefine Western Europe. Although churches were being reopened after the dark days of the Reign of Terror, the Roman Catholic Church in France that baptized Lacordaire was under the total control of the state, as stated in the Concordat of 1801 between Pope Pius VII and Napoleon. Lacordaire would spend most of his life working to restore full freedom to the evangelizing mission of the church in France.

Lacordaire's mother struggled to provide for the education of her four sons and to rear them in the Catholic faith after the death of their father in 1806. Although she was eminently successful in educating her sons, she would be disappointed that Lacordaire and his three brothers, like so many young men of the time, stopped practicing their faith and became deists, following the example of Jean Jacques Rousseau (1712–1778).

After studying law at Dijon and Paris, Lacordaire, a successful young lawyer, had a conversion experience in 1824 that led him to go to confession at the Cathedral of Notre Dame in Paris and to return to the practice of the Catholic faith. Six months later he decided to become a priest. After completing his theological studies at the Grand Séminaire, he was ordained a priest for the Archdiocese of Paris in 1827. Lacordaire was assigned to serve as chaplain at the convent of the Visitation nuns as well as assistant chaplain at the Collège Henri IV. However, dissatisfied at the lack of freedom that the church in France was experiencing, he chose in 1830 to accept an offer from Bishop John

Dubois of New York to become Vicar General of the diocese and rector of the seminary. However, Lacordaire's future ministry was not going to be in the United States.

The July Revolution of 1830, which brought Louis Philippe to the throne of France, seemed to offer new possibilities of greater freedom for the church, for the press, and for education. Hence Lacordaire changed his mind about accepting Bishop Dubois' offer. Instead he remained in Paris and joined Felicité Lamennais, a French priest and author, and Charles Montalembert, a young nobleman, in establishing a daily Catholic newspaper, *L'Avenir*, which carried the motto: "God and Liberty." The collaborative publishing efforts of the three friends lasted for only thirteen months because of the growing opposition of the French bishops to the liberal views *L'Avenir* was supporting. The help they hoped to obtain from a visit to Pope Gregory XVI was not forthcoming, and the three friends chose to follow separate paths.

Lacordaire returned to France and began a ministry of writing and lecturing that led to an invitation from the Archbishop of Paris to give a series of conferences at Notre Dame Cathedral in 1835–1836. In these very popular conferences, which drew huge crowds and made Lacordaire famous, he began a new evangelization of the French people. As he was invited to give conferences in other parts of France in 1837–1838, he found himself at a turning point in his spiritual journey. He believed that he was being called to join his preaching ministry to life in a religious order. His search would culminate in his decision in 1838 to enter the Dominicans and to reestablish the Order in France.

The Dominican Order in the first half of the nineteenth century was in the midst of great crisis. Most of the European provinces were either extinct or in turmoil because of the French Revolution and the empire building of Napoleon Bonaparte. Lacordaire's entry into the Dominican novitiate at La Quercia near Viterbo, Italy in 1839 marked the beginning of a new chapter in the history of the Order in Europe. After his profession of solemn vows in 1840, Lacordaire returned to France in 1843 and opened the first Dominican house since the suppression of the Order in 1790 at Nancy. Lacordaire became the first Provincial of the restored Province from 1850 until 1854. He served as Provincial again from 1858 to 1861.

In 1850 Pope Pius IX named Vincent Jandel, one of Lacordaire's first disciples, Vicar General of the Order. Five years later Pius appointed him Master General of the Order. From the time he became a Dominican, Jandel had disagreed with Lacordaire on the process of restoring the life and mission of the Order. Lacordaire opted for adherence to the Constitutions but held that they needed to be adapted to contemporary conditions. Jandel wanted strict fidelity to the Constitutions of 1690. Both looked to the original inspiration and traditions of the Order, but they disagreed on which customs were necessary and which were now obsolete. The varying visions of these two great Dominicans would be important for the future development of the Order.

While engaged in establishing five Dominican priories between 1843 and 1853, Lacordaire continued his preaching ministry at Notre Dame in Paris from 1844 to 1851. In 1852 he founded a Third Order community of men to teach in the college he was overseeing at Sorèze near Lyons during his second term as Provincial. He died at Sorèze in 1861. The legacy of Lacordaire is to be found both in his efforts to refound the Dominican Order in the nineteenth century and in his struggle to restore full freedom to the evangelizing mission of the church in France through the separation of church and state. The selection that follows is taken from Lacordaire's *Essay on the Re-Establishment in France of the Order of Friars Preachers,* which he wrote in 1839 just before his entry into the Order.

Thomas C. McGonigle, O.P.

From *Essay on the Re-Establishment in France of the Order of Friars Preachers*

How different is the life of a sincere young man who has given his heart and his gifts to God in a religious order. He is poor, but poverty shelters him from destitution. Destitution is a punishment, but poverty is a blessing. He is subject to a rule which is somewhat hard on the body, but in return he receives great liberty of spirit. He has masters who have gone before him in his way of life and who are not his rivals. He makes his appearance in public opportunely, when his thought is mature, without having yet lost the exuberance of youth. His setbacks are comforted, his successes protected against the pride which sullies all glory. He flows along like a river which loves its banks and is not uneasy about its course. How many times, during the hard years which we have just been through, has our fancy dwelt longingly in those peaceful fortresses which have soothed so many passions and shielded so many lives! Now that we have passed the age of storms, it is less for ourselves than for others that we wish to prepare a refuge. Our existence is settled, we have reached the shore; those whom we leave out on the high seas under less favourable winds than ours will understand our hopes and will perhaps respond to them.

If anyone asks us why we have chosen the Order of Friars Preachers we shall answer that it is the one which best suits our nature, our mind and our goal. It suits our nature by its system of government, our mind by its doctrines, and our goal by the means with which it operates, principally preaching and theological science. We certainly do not intend our choice to imply any criticism of any other order. We admire them all. We have present to our mind a letter from pope Clement IV to a knight who had consulted him to find out whether he should take the habit of the Friars Preachers or that of the Friars Minor: "Clement, bishop, servant of the servants of God, to our dear son, a knight, greeting and our apostolic benediction. You ask us for counsel which you could find equally well in yourself. If the Lord has inspired you to leave the world for a better life, we neither wish nor are we able to place any obstacle in the way of God's Spirit, especially since you have a son, well brought up, we feel sure, who will know how to provide for your household. If, persevering in your plan, you ask us whether you should choose the Friars Preachers or the Friars Minor, we leave that to your conscience. For you can find out for yourself the observances followed by the two orders, which are not alike in everything and which surpass each other in different ways. One order has harder beds, a more uncomfortable nakedness, and, as some believe, a more absolute poverty. In the other the food is more frugal, the fasts longer, and, as some maintain, the discipline more holy. So we do not prefer one to the other, but we think that both, founded on strict poverty, tend towards the same end, namely the salvation of souls. Therefore, whether you select the one or the other, you will be taking the narrow road and you will enter through the small door into the land of honey and spaciousness. So weigh them up attentively, examine carefully which one is the more pleasing to your mind, in which you feel confident of doing better and attach yourself to that one, but in such a way as not to withdraw your love from the other one. For the Friar Preacher who does not love the Minors is execrable, and the Friar Minor who hates or despises the Order of Preachers is execrable and damnable. Given at Perugia, April 19th, in the second year of our pontificate.

Pope Clement IV's sentiments here are our own. We have chosen the order which "is the more pleasing to our mind, in which we feel confident of doing better," without denying anyone the love and respect we owe to all orders.

You may perhaps ask why we have chosen to re-establish an old order rather than to found a new one. We shall give two answers. First, the grace to be the founder of an order is the highest and most exceptional that God gives to his saints, and it has not been given to us. And secondly, if God were to grant us the power to create a new religious order, we are sure that, after much reflection, we should discover nothing newer or more adapted to our time and its needs than the rule of St. Dominic. Nothing about it is old except its history, and we should see no need to torment our mind simply for the pleasure of dating from yesterday. St. Dominic, St. Francis of Assisi and St. Ignatius, in adapting the religious state to the propagation of the gospel by teaching, have exhausted all the basic combinations in which this adaptation could be expressed. You might produce new habits and new names, but you will not change the real nature of these three celebrated societies. If the history of the Friars Preachers is vulnerable to certain objections in the minds of our contemporaries, the same is true of the history of the church at large. All you have to do to incur this kind of objection is survive through two epochs, and that which does not survive will always hold what does survive to account for a whole host of things, and the best reply is simply to go on surviving. Things go on surviving only because of certain hidden changes which leave the past in the past and proceed into the future by way of harmony with the present. So it is with the church and with religious orders, as it is with all living bodies which preserve an unchanging identity even while, because of the very progress of life, they undergo a process of change which continually renews them. The church today is identically the same as that of the Middle Ages by its hierarchy, its dogmas, its rituals, its morals. And yet how different it is! It is exactly the same with religious orders and, in particular, with the Friars Preachers. To raise the past as an objection against anyone is to make his cradle an objection to a grown man, to make life an objection to life.

Rose Hawthorne Lathrop (1851–1926)

Rose Hildegarde Hawthorne was born in Lenox, Massachusetts in 1851, third child of the American author Nathaniel Hawthorne and his wife, Sophia Peabody Hawthorne. Rose's father had just published *The Scarlet Letter* and was about to publish *The House of Seven Gables,* and Hawthorne's friend Herman Melville had dedicated his now-famous book *Moby Dick* to him.

Rose was apparently born surrounded by fame and success, but the literary life was not always kind to her father. The family moved to follow his various jobs and opportunities elsewhere in Massachusetts, in England, France, and Italy before returning to Concord, Massachusetts in 1860, when Rose was nine years old. After her father's death in 1864, Rose, her mother, her brother Julian, and her sister Una moved first to Germany and then to England. In Germany Rose first met her brother's friend—and her future husband—George Parsons Lathrop, in 1868.

Rose was twenty when she married George Lathrop. Their only child, Francie, was born in 1876 and died five years later. Their unhappy marriage teetered on the brink of emotional and financial collapse until Rose left George in 1895. He died in 1898 (his death certificate lists chronic nephritis) and there are intimations in her correspondence that George was an alcoholic. It is probable that she obtained a separation of the bond of marriage (without an annulment) from the church prior to his death. Both Rose and her husband had converted to Catholicism in 1891.

Rose sought out other women whose lives of prayer had led them to ministry. Rose also visited the Grey Nuns of the Sacred Heart in Montreal, made a retreat near Boston with the Sisters of Charity of Halifax, and consulted the Madames of the Sacred Heart. By 1896 Rose had trained as a nurse at the New York Cancer Hospital and begun her apostolate to the poorest and most destitute sufferers of cancer in the Lower East Side of Manhattan. She wrote in September 1896: "I took a street car anxiously one day, a Sunday, in order to hunt for the region of the City which should strike me as the best fitted for my attempt at nursing among the poor."

To help support her work she published *Memories of Hawthorne* (1897), a book about her father, whose works by then had gained great popularity. She began her work in two simple rooms on Scammel Street in downtown Manhattan, and needed more space almost immediately. Along with Alice Huber, a successful portrait painter who joined her in 1898 in search of a life of "perfect charity," Rose took in a dying woman, Mrs. Daly, from St. Vincent Ferrer parish in New York City to their own simple lodging on Water Street, also downtown. Meanwhile, the death of her husband left her freer to pursue a religious vocation. She cut her hair and adopted a quasi-religious habit, which New York's Archbishop Corrigan refused her permission to wear. He insisted she interview with the "Women of Calvary," a group of ministering widows on the West Side of Manhattan, but she knew immediately her call was not with them.

The following year Rose and Alice opened St. Rose's Free Home at 426 Cherry Street, in downtown New York City, and as other women joined Rose in her work she sought to create a community into which the sick might come in their final days. Archbishop Corrigan asked her to consider the charisms of well-established orders, so she read about the Franciscans and probably others. She also knew of the Paulists, the Redemptorists, and the Jesuits, all active in New York at the time. When Dominican Father Clement M. Thuente, then assigned to St. Vincent Ferrer, visited them to thank them for their care of his parishioner, Mrs. Daly, he suggested they join the Third Order of St. Dominic, like St. Rose of Lima, whose statue was in their quarters.

Rose's devotion to the sick poor of the city was total, but she kept up with her family as best she could. Around 1898 she wrote to her brother Julian's eldest child, her niece and namesake Hildegarde, that the pressures of service, the rule she was already following in the house, and the permanent affiliation with a religious order kept her from writing earlier: "Also, I have had to plan & scurry about a little, in order to settle the matter of our affiliation with some Order. A Franciscan priest who . . . is a good friend, urged me to join that Order, & we had to read up about it. The Archbishop desires us to decide something soon, & we are ourselves breathless to reach a home." She signs the letter "Your own devoted Rose Hildegarde."

Her own determinations and the influence of Dominican Father Thuente eventually led her to formally adopt the Dominican charism in 1899, and on December 8, 1900, Rose Hawthorne and Alice Huber pronounced vows. Rose took the name Sister Alphonsa; Alice took the name Sister Rose. Archbishop Corrigan granted them permission to wear the Dominican habit, even though they were Tertiaries, or secular Dominicans, at the time. Six years later the Congregation of St. Rose of Lima formally affiliated with the Dominican Order.

Since that time hundreds of women have joined the Dominican Sisters of Hawthorne and served the poor dying of cancer in their homes in the United States, currently in Atlanta, Georgia; Hawthorne, New York; New York, New York; Philadelphia, Pennsylvania; and St. Paul, Minnesota. The cause for Rose Hawthorne's canonization was formally opened on February 4, 2003.

The two brief excerpts below, from her newsletter *Christ's Poor*, speak to her devotion to the truth and to prayer, through which she sustained her devotion to the dying poor.

Phyllis Zagano

From *Christ's Poor*

October, 1901

> In the very midst of the weedy confusion of grossness and dissipation and cruelty, there springs up a sudden and unexplained flower of perfect loveliness, or a strong growth of sterling, manly quality. Over all the sin there often rests a beautiful atmosphere which God permits, to ennoble many a scene of life which in the total sweep is obnoxious. There are days when we exclaim how much God has given to human nature which He will never permit it to lose; that it is not so inexplicable that Christ delighted to be with the sons of men, and that there is no wonder that in spite of His tears, He thought it worth while to remember the ideal aspect of souls who could sin so much. We explain the love of God for the poor by His love for Peter, the grandeur of whose faith was made strong through the weakness of his denials of Christ. The poor can do and feel heroic things.

***

April, 1904

Reflections of a Conscience

It is beyond words comfortable to sink into an easy-chair in a pretty room, with fancy-work close at hand and an amusing book open before us, and no doubt something piquantly sweet in a bon-bon box not far off. How the time flies along when we are amusing ourselves with being at ease! We often say we have not time to do the few things which we set out to do; life seems to be melting like frost-forests from a window-pane. Of course, busy folk sometimes wonder at the amount of labor an hour will hold. It is true, our eyes grow heavy when we are only contented; and if people tell us there are spots on the sun which do not belong there, we are ready to believe them, the universe seems to be so ill managed. Just think! While we are lounging, there are women working; not only those who work for their own living, but those who work for the living of others—in the household, in charity, in reform and mental advancements. Some of these active sisters are blessed with youth, ardor and charm, but they are also blessed with generous devotion. Some of them are growing old, are worn with pitiless waves of fatigue, and are wholly unexpectant of reward in this world. But there is a distinction which seems to point to the satisfaction of these mothers, misses, teachers, students, friends—their eyes are clear and steady and bright. The woman who makes an effort is the woman who is refreshing, even if for a moment she stops to catch her breath, with her hand on her hip. When she enters a room and fixes her eyes upon us, splendid, no matter of what color or shape, we wish to know where she found the elixir which escaped us in our easy-chair, and we sniff for it, but without much result, be the air of our bourdoir the incense of violets themselves. People of energy are a good deal of a mystery to us lazy ones. I think they may be always waging war with a desire to be selfish, and it is the constant struggle which gives them their fine soldierly presence.

Nevertheless, our active sisters enjoy the work they undertake; but with a joy which would seem like suffering to the reclining ones. There seems to be a holy touch laid upon the heads of those who try to be useful in however humble a field. The difficult moment of an effort is the first spring; it is like a fairy leap, and so much follows that we marvel at the powerful worlds within the world. We realize that the universe is very much and very well managed, from the sphere of the "ten righteous men" to the sphere of the planets. Disappointment and unkindness cannot daunt the devoted one who is beginning to live truly, though she may tremble, weep and sink down in secret. She will be up and on before we know it. The awakening of her perceptions which came with a desire to be a servant to the greatest good, shows her what she can never forget—shows her the need for even one more life. She may receive much disciplinary training; but so do the awkward volunteers in the army, whom their country honors and depends upon in her extremity. As for the feeling that we need rest, rest, rest, it is often a fallacious one. It is action which makes muscle. The spirit of life enters into us when we take a vital part in to-day. Often we suffer from rest. A change of occupation is what we most need, as a rule, and the relief hours of an active person turn out to be very intelligent. We must rest, but we need not lose our electricity, which the will, the thought, can command at all times, and which ought to be on guard, like an orderly, to summon us when we should become alert. Headaches evaporate if we must exert ourselves for those we love, or we almost forget the pain, which is the same thing; the ill-temper cannot flourish unless we have idleness in which to reflect upon the motes belonging to some one else. With energy leading the way, ennui lifts from the horizon, and we see color and distance again. There are women who labor day by day in hunger and despair. It seems as if others might labor in comfort and health, instead of sitting down to lassitude and sighs.

But if one's banner bears a grand motto, it is very true that it will take our life-blood to protect it, in the contest with our meaner desires and the other forces arrayed against the health and energy of the world. Still, our life-blood could not be expended to greater advantage.

Georges-Yves Congar (1904–1995)

Georges-Yves Congar was born at Sedan in the French Ardennes in 1904. His middle-class parents were devout and intelligent Catholics. As a child, he grew up with many Protestant and Jewish friends.

In 1921 Congar entered the major seminary in Paris to begin his studies for the priesthood. Here he attended lectures by the great Thomist scholar Jacques Maritain (1882–1973) and Maritain's spiritual mentor, the Dominican spiritual theologian Reginald Garrigou-Lagrange (1877–1964). The influence of both Maritain and Garrigou-Lagrange brought Congar to a deep appreciation of St. Thomas Aquinas and the Dominican tradition. In 1925 he decided to enter the Order of Friars Preachers at the novitiate house of the Province of France at Amiens.

After his novitiate Congar went to the Dominican House of Studies of the Province of France, Le Saulchoir. His studies in philosophy and theology were enriched by Etienne Gilson (1884–1979), a French Catholic historian of philosophy who gave Congar a historical view of the work of St. Thomas Aquinas, and the Dominican scholar Marie-Dominique Chenu (1895–1990), who sought to apply the teachings of St. Thomas to the theological and spiritual needs of the twentieth century. Chenu urged Congar to concentrate on ecumenical studies.

After his ordination to the priesthood in 1930 Congar was sent to Germany to study Lutheranism. When he returned to France he studied French Protestant theology and Eastern Orthodox theology. He also took an active interest in the relationship between the Roman Catholic Church and the Anglican Church. In 1937, while he was teaching full time at Le Saulchoir, Congar wrote a significant work entitled *Divided Christendom* in which he sought to present a Catholic vision of ecumenism that respected the efforts that were currently being made by Protestant and Eastern Orthodox Christians.

Congar was called to serve as a chaplain in the French army in 1940. He was captured by the Germans and was imprisoned at Colditz from 1940 to 1945. His years spent as a prisoner of war with Christians of other traditions further deepened his commitment to the search for Christian unity.

After the war Congar returned to France and resumed his teaching and ecumenical work, but in 1947 he found himself under a cloud of suspicion in the eyes of Roman authorities for his writings on ecumenism. Following his publication of *True and False Reform in the Church* in 1950 and *Lay People in the Church* in 1953, Congar was removed from the faculty of Le Saulchoir in 1954 and sent first to the École Biblique in Jerusalem and then to the Dominican house at Cambridge, where his movements were restricted and he was forbidden to write or speak on ecumenical questions. Through the kindness of the Bishop of Strasbourg, Congar was invited to resume his pastoral and theological ministries within that diocese in 1955. Congar later came to speak of these difficult years as the time of "active patience" that prepared him for the work that lay ahead of him in the years to come.

With the election of Pope John XXIII the cloud of suspicion over Congar and other French theologians was lifted. The pope named Congar a theological consultant to the preparatory commission for the Second Vatican Council. At the Council (1962–1965) Congar contributed significantly to a number of documents, in particular the Decree on Ecumenism, the Decree on the Laity, and the Dogmatic Constitution on the Church.

After the Council, Pope Paul VI appointed Congar to the Catholic/Lutheran Commission on Dialogue and also the Pontifical International Theological Commission. In 1985 Pope John Paul II invited him to attend the Extraordinary Synod, which was convoked in order to discuss the impact of the Council over the past thirty years. Unfortunately Congar's health had begun to fail, and he was unable to attend. The Pope further honored Congar in 1994 by naming him a cardinal. He died the following year at the French Veterans Hospital, where he had resided during his last years of illness.

As a Dominican theologian Congar made lasting contributions to the life and ministry of the church in the areas of ecclesiology, pneumatology, the role of the laity, and ecumenism. Congar's ecclesiology understood the church as a pilgrim that journeys through time and is continually animated by the Holy Spirit in its mission to preach the Gospel in a variety of cultures as it moves toward the full realization of

God's reign. Congar's pneumatology maintained that the Holy Spirit was poured out on all members of the Christian community, enabling the risen Christ to act ever anew in the present to build up the church in accord with the needs of every time and place. Congar's vision of the role of the laity, which he first presented in his work *Lay People in the Church* (1953), was one of mediation between the church and the world through their sharing in the threefold office of Christ as prophet, priest, and king that is given to all in baptism. Ecumenism, which was at the heart of Congar's ministry throughout his life, was the attempt to find a reconciled diversity that could be the basis for Christian unity.

The life and ministry of Yves Congar stand as a profound witness to Dominic's vision of preaching the Gospel to people of all times and places as a source of ever new life and hope. The selections that follow are taken from Congar's *I Believe in the Holy Spirit* (1979); *Diversity and Communion* (1982); and *Called to Life* (1985).

Thomas C. McGonigle, o.p.

From *I Believe in the Holy Spirit*

One of the most important ways in which the Holy Spirit has been restored to the pneumatological ecclesiology of the Council was in the sphere of charisms. This meant that the Church is built up not only by institutional means but also by the infinite variety of the gifts that each person 'has the right and duty to use in the Church and in the world for the good of mankind and for the upbuilding of the Church . . . in the freedom of the Holy Spirit who "breathes where he wills" (Jn 3:8): at the same time, they must act in communion with their brothers in Christ and especially with their pastors.' A new theology, or rather a new programme of 'ministries,' giving the Church a new face that is quite different from the one that the earlier pyramidal and clerical ecclesiology presented, has developed since the Second Vatican Council on the basis of these charisms used for the common good and the building up of the Church. I have discussed this question elsewhere and shall not repeat here what I have already said. I will show in Volume II why it is important and under what conditions it is possible to call the Spirit, who makes the Church by these means, 'co-institutive' of the Church. Going beyond all legal provisions, the Holy Spirit is entrusted with the task of making sure that 'the form of government established by Christ the Lord in his Church' is unfailingly observed.

The Spirit 'blows where he wills.' He is an 'event.' The Council recognized this aspect of the Holy Spirit and placed it within its proper context. The social structures are, for example, at the service of the Spirit. He makes the gospel a contemporary reality and enables men today to understand the Word of God. He prompts developments in the religious life and, in the case of apostolic or missionary initiatives, 'often anticipates the action of those whose task it is to rule the life of the Church.' It is also to the Spirit that the Council attributed the perpetual renewal that the Church has to undergo if it is to be faithful to its Lord—as we might well expect from the Council of the *aggiornamento*. The Council was also anxious that ecumenical endeavour should continue, 'without prejudging the future inspiration of the Holy Spirit.' The whole ecumenical movement, the Council believed, came in the first place from the Holy Spirit, who is also at work in the other Christian communities.

At the same time as giving a higher value to the charisms and in conjunction with this renewed emphasis, the Council also reassessed the importance of the local churches. Karl Rahner was of the opinion that the most valuable new element introduced by the Council was the idea of the local church as the realization of the one, holy, Catholic and apostolic Church. It was defined as such by the Council and both these definitions include an affirmation that the people of God called and gathered together in this way is in fact called 'in the Holy Spirit.' The Church as a whole is presented as a communion of churches, with the Holy Spirit as the principle of that communion. This is very clear from the conciliar texts. A theology of the catholicity of the Church that seeks to express some of the aspects of the Orthodox *sobornost* is outlined in *Lumen Gentium* 13: 'In virtue of this catholicity each individual part of the Church contributes through its special gifts to the good of the other parts and of the whole Church. Thus through the common sharing of gifts and through the common effort to attain fullness in unity, the whole and each of the parts receive increase.' The 'sacred Tradition' is preserved by the 'entire holy people united with their shepherds,' who share in the prophetic functions of Christ. The Council even went so far as to state: 'The body of the faithful as a whole, anointed as they are by the Holy One (cf. Jn 2:20, 27), cannot err in matters of belief. Thanks to a supernatural sense of the faith which characterizes the people as a whole, it manifests this unerring quality . . . .' As Ignace Ziadé, the

Maronite Archbishop of Beirut, said: 'The Church is the mystery of the pouring out of the Spirit in the last times.'

If the fullness that must be recapitulated in Christ is preceded by a material preparation in the history of this world, then the Spirit must already be active in history. Several times in different documents, the conciliar Fathers speak of the Spirit of the Lord 'who fills the whole earth, who . . . directs the unfolding of time and renews the face of the earth (and) is not absent from this development' and who works on man and turns him towards God. The same constitution on the Church in the Modern World also insists that the Spirit makes a new creature of the Christian, but neither this affirmation nor the others referring to the Spirit are developed in the document.

It is therefore possible to say that there are signs of a true pneumatology in the teachings of the Second Vatican Council. The Council provided the texts, but the truth of that pneumatology has to be confirmed in the life of the Church. The whole people of God knows that it has the task of building up the Church and that lay people have to contribute their gifts or charisms to this task. The local churches are still looking for ways of life that are peculiar to them. The chapter on conciliarity that was opened by Vatican II has not yet been brought to an end. There have been many crises, but there have also been generous initiatives. The Catholic Renewal which began in Pittsburgh in the U.S.A. in 1967 and which has spread throughout the world is clearly part of this living pneumatology, since the Spirit is undoubtedly experienced in that movement, at least according to the testimony of those who follow it. Is it perhaps the response to the expectation of a new Pentecost that Pope John XXIII expressed more than once in connection with the Council? It is at least part of that response, but the total response is much greater and much more mysterious. The entire life of the Church is unfolding in the breath of the Spirit of Pentecost.

Pneumatology, like ecclesiology and theology as a whole, can only develop fully on the basis of what is experienced and realized in the life of the Church. In this sphere, theory is to a great extent dependent on praxis. Paul VI brought to a close the Council inaugurated by John XXIII and repeated his predecessor's desire for a new Pentecost. Some years after the close of the Council, he was able to say: 'The Christology and especially the ecclesiology of the Second Vatican Council should be followed by a new study and a new cult of the Holy Spirit, as an indispensable complement of the conciliar teaching.' With these words, then, I will close this volume, since they to a very great extent justify the attempt that I make in the rest of this work to provide such a pneumatology.

From *Diversity and Communion*

Tradition and Traditions

The member churches of the World Council have become aware that although they have the same orientation on scripture and an equal concern to make it the norm of their dogma and their lives, they still have different confessions of faith, liturgies, ecclesiastical structures and theologies. Thirty years ago, Paul Evdokimov wrote: 'Catholics, Protestants, Orthodox, we are all grouped round the Bible. The closed Bible unites us; as soon as we open its pages, the open Bible disunites us. We read it differently, we read different truths in it.' Perhaps that goes too far, because today there is quite a large degree of agreement at an exegetical level. However, it remains true that no church lives by scripture pure and simple. Each church lives by scripture in and through a certain tradition. The awareness of this fact, made explicit from the time of the Third World Conference of Faith and Order, held at Lund from 15–28 August 1952, even led to the formation of a commission to study the question of tradition. This commission published a provisional report in 1961: *The Old and the New in the Church.* Then the two sub-commissions or sections, one North American and the other European, each produced a very interesting preparatory report for the Fourth World Conference of Faith and Order, held at Montreal from 12 to 26 July 1963.

These reports are a landmark. They have expressed a vivid awareness of the historical character of the church, with its two aspects of continuity and newness. Christianity did not begin in the sixteenth century; it has been handed down since Christ and Pentecost. Equally, the reports have demonstrated the need to reconsider relations between scripture and tradition. They criticized the slogan *scriptura sola.* At the same time (November 1962) these questions were discussed at Vatican II; Fr. R. Rouquette could write that the vote taken there on 20 November marked the end of the Counter-Reformation.

The synthesis aimed at for the Montreal conference had been prepared for by a Faith and Order document (no. 40, Geneva 1963).

It is the Montreal Report which is of interest to us. It analysed and sharpened up the distinctions, suggested by the reports, between three understandings of the word tradition:

The content of Tradition (with a capital T) is 'the revelation of God and the gift which he has made of himself in Christ, his presence in the life of the church' by the power of the Holy Spirit (nos. 45, 46). Scripture is the written form or the written testimony to this (no. 50).

By contrast, tradition (with a small t) is the fact of the transmission of Tradition (no. 46). Catechetical teaching is an essential vehicle of it (no. 74), but so too are the word and the sacraments (no. 56 end). 'Tradition can be a faithful transmission of the Gospel, but it can also disfigure it' (no. 48).

The traditions 'are the expressions and manifestations under different historical forms of the one truth and the one reality which is Christ' (no. 47). These historical expressions and forms characterize the different 'confessions' or existing groups: there is the Presbyterian tradition, the pietistic tradition, the Roman tradition, and so on. So the word can designate either the form of expression or the 'confession' which hands it on and is characterized by it (no. 47). It is clear that geographical, ethnic, historical and cultural elements find their way into these specific expressions which are characteristic of a group, being conveyed through history and seeing to the continuance of the group. These traditions are in fact the specific vehicle of Tradition: they can transmit it all. That this happens in the case of fundamental matters is the basis for a Christianity common to all the communions, the fact which makes ecumenism possible. However, should we not recognize that all the churches, in their specific and historical reality, are incomplete realizations and expressions of Tradition? That applies even to the Orthodox Church and to the Roman Catholic Church. That is also the basis and the appeal of ecumenism.

What will be the criterion for the fidelity of tradition and traditions to the Tradition? The Montreal Conference identified it as scripture (no. 49), the scriptures correctly interpreted. But what is 'correct interpretation' (no. 51)? 'The question of interpretation arises as soon as one resorts to written documents' (no. 49). 'This problem has been regarded in various ways by the different churches' (no. 53), a statement which is followed by the main approaches. This is too complex a question to be discussed in a few words, and in any case it is not directly relevant.

By contrast, I would want to keep one of the expressions relevant to the theme of this book: diversity in a degree of unity. In ecumenism I constantly welcome the expression that 'the others' make the traditions in which they live out Christianity. And we make our starting point the division between elements of doctrine and 'non-theological' (ethnic, historical and cultural) themes of division. The report of the American section commented here:

> Pluralism is evident throughout the history of the church. The diversity of traditions must be recognized, even when the integrity of the Tradition is professed. This diversity cannot be eliminated by a simplistic return to New Testament Christianity, to the *consensus quinquesaecularis,* to the Vincentian canon or to an elementary paradigm, like the idealization of the thirteenth or sixteenth centuries. No tradition of itself has the authority to disinherit the others. All have a fundamental right to be examined in the light of the intention that they profess to obey the tradition.

That is the dossier, the challenge or the paradox of ecumenism. It is on the move towards the final eschatological revelation and communion. An impossible task? It is enough to know that we are summoned to perform it. That is a necessity.

From *Called to Life*

In the Spirit and in fire

"Love never ends." Here on earth, it is true, it does not enjoy the beatific transparence and absolute self-giving that knows no limitation of space and time, but its nature as a principle of communion is already in evidence and it is already rooted in the Holy Spirit. "God's love has been poured out into our hearts through the Holy Spirit who has been given to us" (Rom 5, 5). Both the *Ecumenical Bible* and the *Jerusalem Bible* point out that this text is speaking of the love which is God's own and with which he loves us. Thus we are already endowed with the very principle on which heaven rests. We are already that new creation which must renew this world in which we are now living and bring it to fulfillment (cf. Gal 6, 15; 2 Cor 5, 17; Rom 6, 4 and 7, 6). But that life is "hid with Christ in God. When Christ our life appears, then you also will appear with him in glory" (Col 3, 3; Eph 2, 19; 1 Jn 3, 1-2). We are still living here on earth in the flesh (cf. 2 Cor 10, 3) but, in and through Christ, we live the life of the children of God.

To take up the categories set out by Origen, we can rightly say that the origin and end, which correspond to each other, are present in the milieu in which our present life is spent. But they are hidden. Only those who know and love God are aware of them and they here and now give thanks to God. These people are the priests of the creation, the interpreters of the sighs with which, as the Scriptures say, creation awaits the revelation of God.

Perfect communion which overcomes the divisions of space and time is, like its source, the Holy Spirit, an eschatological reality. But like the Holy Spirit that communion is given as an earnest. Its perfect bond is charity, love (cf. Col 3, 14). Love brings others into my life. It makes them present to me despite the distance that may separate them from me. Love even now bridges the gaps made by space and time and, indeed, unites all those whom Christ has reconciled "whether on earth or in heaven" (Col 1, 20). It is, in truth, because of Christ and through the Holy Spirit that that which will be achieved perfectly and in full light in heaven has already its beginning here on earth, in the Mystical Body. Because "in Christ the whole fulness of deity dwells" (Col 2, 9), he can be all in all and bring about that God is here and now "through all and in all" (Eph 4, 6). Out and beyond what we ourselves can see, which is in the sphere of history and geography (space and time), the catholicity of the Body of Christ remains a mystery: "I believe in the catholic Church." The great Scholastics, in commenting on these words of the Creed, linked with them the article on the Holy Spirit: I believe in the Holy Spirit who makes the Church one, holy, catholic and apostolic. How the juridical and sociological angles on the Church seem inadequate in the face of this spiritual reality! Nevertheless the provision of genuine community facilities does foster the spiritual ideal of communion at the level of the physical reality of our life in this world.

The world of tangible things is our assigned setting in which we live out our lives, and within it we are in advance in a limited degree, something of a fulfilment of the end for which it has all been created. In this way there exists a continuity between the "here below" and "the world to come." They are not two spheres of existence totally cut off from each other. The phrase "heaven and earth" can serve to indicate two states of one and the same human life while at the same time pointing to the light that one throws on the other, namely, on the one hand the temporal condition of human beings during their earthly existence and on the other hand their condition in eternity.

We have been baptised with the baptism of Jesus Christ, "with the Holy Spirit and with fire" (Mt 3, 11). The Spirit is the source of our communion with one another, for he transcends space and time, inhabits within us, makes us transparently open to one another and enables us to relate to one another in love. It is in the unity of the Holy Spirit that, in heaven and already here on earth, to the Father, with the Son, is rendered all honour and all glory.

Edward Schillebeeckx (1914–   )

The Dominican tradition of scholarship in the service of the church is well understood in the depth and breadth of the work of Dominicans since the first followers of Dominic stepped out to preach eight hundred years ago. The famous Dominicans of history—St. Albert the Great, St. Thomas Aquinas, Meister Eckhart, Catherine of Siena, and many others—have lent their heritage to modern times. Not all were accepted by their contemporaries, but all made large contributions to the ways in which the church thinks about the truth.

Belgian-born Edward Schillebeeckx is one of the world's most prominent theologians. He was born in Antwerp November 12, 1914, the sixth child of Johanna and Constant Schillebeeckx, who would eventually have a family of fourteen children. Schillebeeckx' father was an accountant in the Public Records Office.

Schillebeeckx' older brother entered the Society of Jesus (Jesuits), but Edward entered the Dominicans at nineteen, having determined they better suited his temperament and strengths. He was especially attracted to Dominican dedication to dogmatic theology, particularly the mystery of God, and their interest in social questions. His novitiate at Ghent was followed by compulsory military service, after which he attended the Catholic University of Louvain and was ordained in 1941. He taught theology, and early in his career he worked with Yves Congar. For most of his academic career he was professor of the history of theology at Nijmigen University in the Netherlands.

It is nearly impossible to categorize Schillebeeckx' opus, diverse as it is. He has published over four hundred works in fourteen different languages, and his work has more than once been examined by Vatican authorities. Some of his earlier writing, *Revelation and Theology; Christ, the Sacrament of the Encounter with God;* and *God, the Future of Man* joined the exuberance in the church following the Second Vatican Council, and for a time made him nearly popular. The difficulty of his writing, however, gives clear indication of the depth of his thought.

Schillebeeckx was a private theological advisor to the Dutch episcopacy during the Second Vatican Council. Dutch Cardinal B. J. Alfrink twice failed to have him appointed an official *peritus;* his appointment was prevented by Cardinal Ottaviani, apparently because Schillebeeckx had ghost-written the Dutch bishops' call for *aggiornamento* two years before the Council opened. Nevertheless, he had a great deal of influence in the Council, and his foresight and interest in the reconciliation of the church and the modern world marks him to this day.

The substance of Schillebeeckx' writing and theological thought is far beyond the scope of this small volume, but the very interesting essay he wrote in 1983 on Dominican spirituality that follows well complements it.

Phyllis Zagano

From *Dominican Spirituality*

For the most part people live by stories. I myself live by my own story. When I became a Dominican I linked my life story with the family story of the Dominicans; as a result, my life story took on a new orientation and I picked up the thread of the story of the Order in my own way. So my own life has become part of the Dominican family story: a chapter in it. Through the story of the Order I have attained my own identity. Stories of the Dominican Order keep us together as Dominicans. Without stories we should lose our memories, fail to find our place in the present and remain without hope or expectation for the future. Thus as Dominicans we form a group by virtue of being our own storytelling community, which hands down its own traditions within the wider story of the many religious communities, within the all-embracing story of the great community of the church, and within the even greater community of humankind. This makes us our own special family, recognizable from all kinds of family characteristics. Some are major, some are minor, but none of them can be hidden.

In saying this, I have already said something about Dominican spirituality. The story of my life can be my own life story only in so far as it has become a chapter of the Dominican family story. The story of my own life extends and enriches the history of

Dominican spirituality, while as a small—almost infinitesimally small—chapter in it, it is at the same time relativized and criticized by the already older and wider story of the Dominican family. This makes me ask whether I really am not distorting this family story. So I am already sceptical about all those who would suggest 'one's own insight' or 'one's own experience' to others as a norm for Dominican spirituality. Furthermore, thank God, there are still Dominicans alive today. In other words, our story is not yet exhausted, completely told; there is still something to be said.

A first conclusion already follows from this: a definitive all-round definition of Dominican spirituality cannot be given. You cannot make a final judgment on a story which is still going strong. We can only trace some of the main lines in the plot of the story, which has now been handed down for seven centuries in constantly different ways: the one basic story has been told in countless other languages to constantly different listeners, and has varied depending on their cultural, historical circumstances and the nature of their church.

The basic story which stands at the beginning of our own Dominican storytelling community is of fundamental importance here. But the origin of any relevant story usually blurs into an obscure past which is difficult to reconstruct historically. Dominic (1170–1223), the origin of the Dominican family story, did not write any books. Nevertheless, through laborious historical reconstruction which extracts the 'real Dominic' from all kinds of legends (so typical of the Middle Ages), we have sufficient firm ground under our feet. In particular, though Dominic may not have left behind any books or documents, what he did leave behind as a living legacy was the Dominican movement, the Order, a group of people who wanted to carry on his work in his footsteps. The Dominican story therefore begins with Dominic and his first companions; together they stand at the beginning of what was to become the Dominican family story. They gave the story its theme: they set its tone.

However, this story, often retold and sometimes rewritten, is in itself a particular way in which the thread of an already older story, that of Jesus of Nazareth, is taken up and continued in a new manner. This already brings us to a second conclusion. Dominican spirituality is valid only in so far as it takes up the story of Jesus and brings it up to date in its own way. In its Decree on the Renewal of Religious Life, the Second Vatican Council said that 'to follow Jesus' is the ultimate and supreme norm of any form of religious life (*suprema regula,* no. 2). Dominican spirituality is therefore subject to the criterion of the sources of all Christian life. This also means that even the Dominican spirituality of Dominic and his first followers is not directly an absolute law for Dominicans. A fuller and more sophisticated knowledge of the story of Jesus which has become possible since then (e.g. through new devotional experiences based on the Bible or through more refined exegesis of scripture) may therefore lead us to different emphases from those of Dominic and his followers. For according to the Council's Decree on Religious Renewal, this renewal must happen in the first place through a return 'to the sources of all Christian life' (no. 2), the gospel of Jesus Christ (Mark 1.1). That source is never exhausted and always offers new possibilities, for which even Dominic himself did not know the all-embracing 'Open Sesame.'

At the same time this implies that the story of every religious Order must be judged as a part or, better, as a modulation of the greater story of the 'community of God,' the church ('a participation in the life of the church': ibid., no. 2). Here the Council points to the 'present-day projects' of the church: biblical, liturgical, dogmatic, pastoral, ecumenical, missionary and social. That is, Dominican spirituality essentially presupposes a critical involvement in the very specific needs and problems of today's church in its historical circumstances; it cannot be an isolated cultivation of our own 'Dominican' garden alongside the ongoing life of the world and the church.

Given all this, however, governed by the gospel and subject to the constant historical criticism that it exercises, and at the same time as a concrete historical feature of the necessary major projects of the church in the world here and now, in fact 'the original inspiration of one's own religious institution' (thus the Council's Decree on Religious Life, no. 2) is the basic theme of the Dominican family story, and is therefore normative. Here the Council Decree points not only to the original 'specific project' *(propria proposita)* of the founder, but also to the Order's 'own religious traditions', at least in so far as these are sound *(sanae traditiones)*; that is, to the 'spiritual heritage' of a religious order: its spirituality.

The third conclusion may therefore be that Dominican spirituality is valid as a special mode of the church's task 'to follow Jesus,' especially—for us—in the footsteps and the inspiration of

Dominic, as this inspiration has constantly provided new light and direction in the best moments of the history of the Order. Therefore we must clearly bring this basic historical story to mind, for in the course of time the Dominican community has also had a broken relationship to its own origins. When the Inquisition brought, for example, Joan of Arc to the stake, the Dominicans involved were essentially contradicting Dominic's inspiration and orientation. People had become deaf and blind to the origin of new charismata: this was an essentially un-Dominican attitude.

As a third criterion for renewed religious life, the same Decree of the Council gives the relationship of the story of Jesus and the original basic story (for us, of the Dominicans) to the altered circumstances of the time (no. 22). This implies that Dominican spirituality cannot be defined purely by a reference to the original story or purely by a reference to the further modulations and updating of this basic story in the course of the history of the Order, though this is presupposed. Dominican spirituality also involves the way in which we live out this Dominican family story here and now, in our time. Dominican spirituality does not indicate simply how things were 'at the beginning' or in the course of the history of the Order. In that case we would simply be writing a historical report of the way in which Dominicans were inspired in former times. But historical knowledge is not yet spirituality. Thus someone who was a good historian but not a Dominican could reconstruct it better than we could. If it is not to be purely the 'history' of a spirituality (and furthermore, if it is not to become an empty ideology), Dominican spirituality is a living reality today; it is handed on (or distorted) by Dominicans living now, who reshape the Dominican family story here and now with an eye to the situation in the world and the church, the cultural historical situation of the moment.

Thus the fourth conclusion runs as follows: without a living relationship to the present, any talk about Dominican spirituality remains a purely historical preoccupation with the past of the Order (often an excuse for neglecting tasks which are urgent now). Dominican spirituality is a living reality which is to be realized among us now. Otherwise we simply repeat stories which others have told for a long time, as though we ourselves did not have to write our own chapter in what is of course a story which had already begun before us. Whereas now we do have to write a new chapter that is still unpublished, if after us anyone else is going to think it worth taking up the thread of this Dominican story again. If in fact we can, may and will write that new living chapter, I am certain that many young people, men and women, will again be drawn to continue the Dominican tradition after us. For any meaningful story has a power of attraction; it is retold, and no one can stop its snowball effect. Whether that happens, however, depends on the tone in which we write our chapter in the great Dominican family story and the tension it contains. Will it be a dull, unread little paragraph? Or will it be an alien story which does not take up the thread of the family story that has already begun, and so allows the Dominican story to die out, perhaps for good? Or will it become an attractive episode, attractive perhaps only because all that the hearer notices is that we are zealously in search of the real thread of the story, which for the moment we have lost track of? That too can also be an important part of the already old Dominican family story.

A 'golden thread' runs through the Dominican family story, from Dominic down to the present day. As may become evident, this golden thread sometimes runs across the fabric of Christianity—a fact that we must not obscure when we are writing our share in the great history of the Order. Provided that this golden thread is woven into our life story, however different it may be in content, we have in fact realized Dominican spirituality. 'Spirituality' is not spirituality so long as it is only described, whether in an assertive or an authoritarian tone. It is spirituality to the degree that is realized in practice—as a completely new rendering of an old Dominican melody.

How does this older melody go, this constantly recurring theme, this basic story?

I would say that it is a cross-grained story! In the twelfth century and at the beginning of the thirteenth there were two burning issues: a need for renewal in the priestly life and a need for renewal in the monastic life. The Fourth Lateran Council in 1215 dealt with the two problems separately, without any relation between them, and without connecting the two. This Council was not without its influence on Dominic who, as an Augustinian canon of Osma, on a journey to the south of France had already gathered round him a group of fellow workers to provide for the pressing needs of priestly care in the diocese of Toulouse, which had severe pastoral problems. Dominic saw the signs of the times. In the twelfth century, religious movements had arisen: a great many lay people joined them. The basic tendency of these movements was to combine gospel poverty with preaching, but they often had an anti-clerical tone. All kinds of clerical abuses had prompted the question: does Christian preaching require the permission of the church (the bishop), and involve commissioning and sending by the church? Or is not religious life, and life according to the gospel in the footsteps of the apostles (at that time called the *vita apostolica*), itself a qualification for Christian preaching? This last view was the standpoint of many religious movements, whereas it was officially regarded as 'heresy' by the Councils. We could say that the heretical movements of that time were inspired by the gospel and Christ, while the official preachers, though orthodox, did not lead a life in accordance with the gospel—at least to all outward appearances—and were completely embedded in feudal structures. All manifestations of this new religious movement—above all in France, Italy, Germany and the Netherlands (the rich countries of that time)—show striking common features (independently of each other): living out the gospel *sine glossa* (without compromises). Its spirituality was characterized by a deep devotion to the humanity of Jesus: following the poor Jesus. (This happened under the influence of the Cistercian movement and the Gregorian reform.)

At the same time there was clear influence from the contemplative, Greek Byzantine East (through the Crusaders and cloth merchants). The situation became more serious when these gospel movements came into contact with dualistic Eastern movements which arrived in the West through the Slavonic lands of the Danube; they were called Cathars, a collective term for Gnostic and dualistic trends. As a result the whole of the 'gospel movement' became even more suspect to the church. The problem became that of saving the gospel movement for the church and mobilizing it against heresy. We must set the phenomenon of Dominic against this historical background of all kinds of enthusiastic revivals of evangelism, but on the periphery of the official church. Dominic was not alone in seeing the problems in the situation: Pope Innocent III, Bishop Diego, with whom Dominic travelled to the south, and Francis of Assisi also saw it. With outspoken realism, Dominic formulated a clear rescue programme. He saw that an enormous potential for the gospel was being lost to the church. Though trained in the already traditional canonical priestly life, he was nevertheless sympathetic to these new counter-experiments. But he saw quite clearly why they either kept failing (splitting off into 'heretical' sects), or came to be incorporated once again into traditional monastic life (e.g. the Premonstratensians). He wanted to make these counter-movements authentic alternative forms of the church's evangelism, a church movement: he wanted as it were to 'live like the heretics' but 'teach like the church.'

Evangelism must be a challenge within the church; in other words it must be the church and not a sect. Dominic's own vision came near to this in that he saw the solution of the problems of the time in the combination—in one institution—of apostolic preaching (that is, preaching with a critical remembrance of the need for a proclamation endorsed by the pope or by the episcopate), and the *vita apostolica* (that is, radical evangelism: following Jesus like the apostles). He brought together organically, in one programme, the themes treated separately by the Fourth Lateran Council. Because this same Council, to some extent contrary to the personal views of Pope Innocent III, had forbidden all new forms of religious life and 'banned' unauthorized preaching, Dominic combined the best of traditional monastic life with the basic trends of the new counter-movements which had arisen all over Europe and which, to make the Christian proclamation credible, required a life commensurate with the gospel from those who proclaimed it. In so doing he broke down the feudal structures of the old monastic life: thus there arose a new form of religious life, the Order of Preachers, the Dominicans. Hence our earliest constitutions are largely made up of elements from the constitutions of traditional religious life, especially from the Norbertines and Cistercians (at that time the most lively religious institutions). However, Dominic and his first followers transformed these elements by the very purpose of the Order: apostolic itinerant preaching; that is, the new spirit of what were then modern, experimental gospel movements brought into the perspective of the church.

Dominic had been caught up in this spirit through his contact in the south of France with all this heretical gospel enthusiasm, which was shared by a broad spectrum of people, high and low. Through the structure of his Order, Dominic had weakened the economic stability which had been the basic principle of the older monastic institutions. On the basis of a *religious* criticism Dominic thus attacked the foundations of the feudal system (in church and society). Furthermore, the association of the contemplative monastic element with itinerant preaching resulted in a basic difference from the traditional form of monastic life. The new 'corporative' idea (a particular form of organization, as in the official guilds) was adapted to the religious institution: there was no 'monarchical' authority from above but a democratic form of government with a range of choices (democratic and personal). Paradoxically, Dominic's evangelism led to a new incarnation in secular structures, especially those of the rising democratic mediaeval bourgeoisie.

By thread and cross-thread, Dominic wove a new fabric, created a new religious programme. Thus the Dominican Order was born from the charisma of the combination of admonitory and critical recollection of the spiritual heritage of the old monastic and canonical religious life with the 'modernistic' religious experiment of the thirteenth century. Dominic had a fine sensitivity both to religious values from the past and to the religious promise for the future emanating from the modern experiments of his time. The Dominican Order was born out of this two-fold charisma. I would say that this is our *gratia originalis,* the grace at the origin of our Order.

Dominican spirituality is therefore in the first instance to be defined as a spirituality which, on the basis of admonitory and critical reflection on the heritage left behind by the past religious tradition, takes up critically and positively the cross-thread provided by whatever new religious possibilities for the future keep emerging among us. Therefore it can never be a *material* repetition of what our Dominican forebears have themselves done admirably. Nor, however, can it be an *uncritical* acceptance of whatever 'new movements' (in the mystical or political sense) are now evident in our midst. For Dominic, the essential thing was the question of truth. In his heart Dominic was ultimately one hundred per cent behind the new apostolic experiments of *preaching* combined with poverty, but—remembering the good achievements of the previous patterns of religious life—he unconditionally observed the guidelines laid down by the Fourth Lateran Council (1215) for any renewal of both priestly and religious life. His charisma was organically to combine two divergent guidelines and thus personally to extend the aims of this Council.

On the basis of this spirituality, which found expression in our very first Dominican Constitutions, the further history of the spirituality becomes understandable. This brings the historical, changing, cross-grained, new element into the very heart of Dominican spirituality. For example, the Constitutions from the years 1221–31

said: 'Our brothers may not study the books of pagan writers (referring above all to Aristotle) and philosophers (what is meant is
Arabic philosophy, the great modernism in the Middle Ages); far
less may they study the secular sciences.' However, only about
twenty years later, Albert the Great and Thomas Aquinas were to
regard the study of secular sciences and the 'pagan philosophers'
as a necessary condition of the preparation and formation of an
appropriate Dominican apostolate. Thus on the basis of an authentic Dominican spirituality these two Dominican saints boldly
went against a Dominican constitution set up in earlier times and
were therefore in opposition to what was then in fact called official 'Dominican spirituality.' They did this—inspired by what
Dominic did in his time—so successfully that the definition was
later removed from the Constitutions by a General Chapter; indeed, later Constitutions urged Thomas as a model (Raymond of
Penafort had centres for the study of Arabic built in Nursia and
Tunis). That is an authentically Dominican development, after the
heart of St. Dominic, who himself tried to reconcile 'the past' and
new 'possibilities for the future.' (This brought with it the new
danger that Thomas would later cease to be a beacon pointing towards the future and would become a closed frontier). If no cross-
thread can be seen in the story that the Dominican perceives and
takes up again himself, there is every chance that Dominican spirituality will fade; worse still, that on the basis of an 'established'
Dominican spirituality—which is a contradiction in terms—we
shall wrongly write off as apocryphal talk new attempts at a truly
Dominican spirituality. The greatest moments in the history of our
Order are when at the same time this history becomes anti-history
or a cross-thread: Dominic himself, Albert and Thomas, Savonarola,
Eckhardt, de Las Casas, Lacordaire, Lagrange, Chenu, Congar, to
name a few. However, at the same time Dominicans have sometimes (in the first instance at least) run into difficulties with the already established Dominican story when in an un-Dominican
way it has refused to take up the new cross-thread. Without mis-
taking the fundamental worth, by which we are all supported, of
the many anonymous Dominicans who have quietly lived a successful Dominican religious life (though their tranquillity can
have a broad influence and produce cross-grained stories within
the Order), nevertheless it only becomes clear what is typically
Dominican when Dominicans sometimes, following the example
of Dominic, reshape 'the old' and combine it with the dynamism

of constantly new and different forms. If this does not happen at regular intervals, then there is every chance that the well-known Dominican concern for truth will be dishonoured in an Inquisition and the new 'Dominican possibilities' are rejected. These possibilities may then come to life outside the Dominican family. I would not want to include this less rosy story—which is also part of our Order—in the golden thread of our family story, which is always in a state of constantly taking up the cross-thread again. However, the cross-thread sometimes ensures the continuity! The history of this cross-thread is the golden thread of the Dominican family story, woven into a broader, as it were more serene, whole. That St. Ignatius of Loyola was shut up in the cellars of one of our monasteries because he shocked the people of his time with a new charisma is one of the many stories in which 'Dominican spirituality' has perversely become its opposite; it now shows us to be guilty of un-Dominican chauvinism. In other words, this is typical of times in which the Dominicans were no longer 'Dominican' and on the basis of their own 'established' position had already dubbed the new counter-thread heretical. The constantly new forms which Dominican spirituality must take in accordance with Dominic's basic story will emerge even more clearly, precisely through the moments in which we have failed in the past.

It is essential for Dominican spirituality to attend to God as God has already revealed himself to us in the past and to attend to the present-day 'signs of the time' in which the same God, who is faithful to us, makes his appeal. Any one-sidedness—in one-track, uncritical judgment either of the past or of what prove to be symptoms of the future in the present—is un-Dominican. Dominic submits the present, with its own possibilities of experiment, to comparison with the dangerous recollection of certain events and legacies from the past, just as at the same time he opens up the global past and gives it the stamp of the cross-grained experimental present: it is out of this kind of attitude that the Order was born. This must remain its 'genius.' The *présence à Dieu* and the *présence au monde* (as Lacordaire puts it) describe the very nature of Dominican spirituality throughout the history of the Order. And perhaps today we are going to see clearly that—in recollection of the religious past—the *présence au monde* or critical solidarity with the human world is the only possible mode of our *présence à Dieu*. At the same time this insight confirms the need for a critical recollection of the religious past in which the same *présence à*

Dieu is always revealed in the communication of what were then the contemporary signs of the time. The 'modernism' of the Dominican Order lives on dangerous memories from the past. After what was almost a centuries-long sleep, Père Lacordaire and Master General Jandel were the ones who in the nineteenth century recalled the Dominican Order to its original charisma and brought about a break with the serene traditionalism to which the 'established order' had succumbed. 'Lacordaire' (and everything connected with that within our Dominican history) was in fact the rediscovery of the Order by itself. For the Lacordaire movement was nourished by the original charisma of the Order and as a result again raised the problem of 'Dominican spirituality.'

Some characteristics of Dominican spirituality are clear from this:

1. Belief in the absolute priority of God's grace in any human action: the theological direction of the Dominican life and its programme in relation to ethics, the world, society and the betterment of people. There must be no obsessive concern with the self but trust in God: I can trust God more than myself. The result is a tranquil and happy spirituality. God still gives an unexpected future to the limited meaning and scope of my own actions.

2. Religious life in the light of the gospel *(vita apostolica)* as the atmosphere in which the Dominican is *apostolic (salus animarum,* salvation as the aim of the activity of the Order): through preaching in all its forms. The result of that is *contemplari* and *contemplate aliis fradere* (i.e. the agreement between what a person proclaims and his own life; here Thomas Aquinas is contrasting the character of the mendicants with that of other religious institutions and at the same time connecting this with 'poverty': being free from financial worries). This general mendicant view became typically Dominican through the insertion of study as an essential element into the structure of this Dominican evangelism. This particular element was not characteristic of the mediaeval evangelical movements. 'Study is not the aim of the Order but an essential instrument for this work' (says Humbert of Romans in his commentary on the Constitutions). The failure of many gospel movements was also caused by a lack of thought. Furthermore, while the universities, which were only established at that time, had intensified the element of academic study, at the same time they had concentrated it and centralized it so that there were no intellectuals in the dioceses. Dominic saw this, and therefore he incorporated study as an insti-

tutional element in the very organization of his Order. He would not have any monastery founded 'without a doctor in theology,' and every monastery had to be a 'school of theology': a Dominican monastery is 'permanent instruction.' The distinction between study monasteries and pastoral monasteries is un-Dominican; both must be monasteries for study and pastoral ministry. Thomas Aquinas defended a religious institution 'founded for study.'

3. The 'Jesus spirituality' of the order—the 'humanity of Jesus' (Albert, Thomas, Eckhardt, Tauler, Susa, etc., here directly connected with the only two Dominican devotions, to Mary and to Joseph), but this humanity experienced as a personal manifestation of God's joy for humankind—is the centre of Dominican spirituality and mysticism without any predilection for 'derivative devotions.' All this is typical of the twelfth century; along with all the other characteristics it is also typically Dominican.

4. *Présence au monde* (*la grâce d'entendre ce siècle,* as Père Lacordaire says): openness for constantly new charismata which different circumstances require of us. Hence the need for structures which do not hem us in but are democratic and flexible, through which it becomes possible for Dominicans to accept the rise of new stories that go against the grain. It is characteristic that the Dominicans never had their Constitutions approved by the pope, so that they themselves could adapt them to new circumstances.

5. (As a consequence of 4.): Since Albert and Thomas, Dominican spirituality has been inwardly enriched by the inclusion of the Christian principle of secularization within the essentially religious, gospel trend (Dominicans at first rejected this, but soon they generally accepted it). This involves first coming to know things (objects, inter-personal relationships, society) in their intrinsic characteristics and their own structures rather than prematurely defining their relationship to God. In modern times this has enormous consequences by comparison with all kinds of forms of pseudo-mystical supernaturalism, which often ends up as a sense of superiority masquerading as piety.

To begin with, the Order agonized over the introduction of 'natural sources' into Dominican evangelism. The traditional rejection of the 'profane sciences' by the monks continued to have an effect, though this was limited by the Dominican principle of dispensation. The first Dominicans were 'anti-philosophical' (thus running the risk of an evangelical supernaturalism). The *Vitae Fratrum* reeked of 'holy naivety.' Albert and Thomas changed the direction, Albert even arguing fiercely against fellow-brethren 'who thus again want to become the murderers of Socrates.' The dispute was over the consequences of integral evangelism, which Albert and Thomas wanted to be enlightened in character, not naive. In the Chapter of Valenciennes (1259), the trend supported by Albert and Thomas won through: the study of the 'profane sciences' became compulsory in Dominican training.

6. The other elements: a liturgical choral office, monastic observances and community life, are traditional and generally religious, and in this sense not typically Dominican. That was the dangerous recollection of the monastic and canonical past to which Dominic continued to give expression in his new religious and apostolic programme, albeit in critical, reduced and more modest form.

7. The 'principle of dispensation' (historically this seems to go back to Dominic himself in person), i.e. respect for the particular personal charisma of a fellow Dominican within the Dominican community, bearing in mind the purpose of the Order. Of course this is an extremely dangerous principle, which has been abused to disastrous effect. However, Dominic would rather take that risk than give up the human and Christian significance of the dispensation principle because of the threat of abuse. As a general principle this was a completely new Dominican discovery in the Middle Ages. In furtherance of study in the service of the 'salvation of men' *(salus animarum)* and in furtherance of the apostolate, it is, paradoxically, possible to be a Dominican (if necessary) on your own. This presupposes having been trained as a Dominican, but it is in no way understood as a matter of standing outside the law: on the contrary, dispensation is a constitutional Dominican law. Conformity is alien to the original Dominican legislation. Even now, this original Dominican principle opens up broad possibilities for 'modern experiments' in our time, even experiments which some people accustomed to an 'established' Dominican spirituality cannot stand. (However, these experiments also always need to happen from and within the dangerous recollection of a tradition which is already centuries old. This tradition prefigures permanent perspectives which are always worth thinking about—without it all experiments seem doomed to religious failure).

Although there are countless examples of this characteristic from our rich family archives, I want to point to just one event in the first redactions of our Dominican Constitutions. The striking 'democratic structure' of our Order has been said by experts in administration to be unique among Catholic monastic institutions. This feature can be understood precisely as a result of the typical cross-grained spirituality of the Order (along with its respect for all that is good in the tradition). The Constitutions were 'reformulated' during a revision at a time when great canon lawyers from the universities of the time had entered the Order (for example, Raymond of Penafort). This reformulation took place at a General Chapter in Bologna. Shortly before and during this Chapter, social protests were voiced in the university and city of Bologna, and in addition there was already a dispute between the Ghibellines (the conservatives) and the Guelphs (the progressive popular party). Dominicans were involved throughout this conflict as advisors. The 'co-responsibility of all' required by the progressive party had its influence on our Dominican Constitutions. 'What affects all must also be resolved on by all.' This new civic principle called for at that time was also supported by the Dominicans and later sanctioned in our Dominican Constitutions (under the influence and as a result of the civic experiences in Bologna). New 'secular experiences' thus came to exercise a substantial influence on our earliest Constitutions. The emancipatory social movements of that time left a substantial mark on our Constitutions, differing completely from the traditional administrative model then current. Following the example of Dominic, these Dominicans did not just raise a warning finger and point to what had been the custom from earliest times, but at the same time listened to the voice of God in what came out of the human secular emancipatory movements of the time (however turbulently). As a result of these experiences they rewrote the Dominican monastic structure, barely twenty years after Dominic. That is just one case of the cross-thread that the Dominican family story keeps showing as its 'own theme' down the ages.

I have recalled only a few Dominican characteristics: more could be mentioned. Furthermore, I should point out explicitly that I am in no way denying that perhaps non-Dominicans do the same things. In that case Dominican spirituality can simply say with delight: all the better! It is not our concern to maintain an unparalleled exclusiveness. It is a question of what we, as Dominicans, do here in any case, and do in the strength of the charisma of the Order and our Dominican commitment (through our profession). If others also do the same thing, this can simply confirm the validity, the correct intuition of our view. When a typical view is universalized, it in no way loses its value: quite the opposite.

The man who was once an Augustinian canon, Domingo de Guzmán, while trusting in the original direction of his life, nevertheless gave it a new course (which became the beginning of the Dominican Order), thanks to a living contact with needs of people and of the church of which he was unaware when he was first called. One cannot accuse Dominic of betraying his first calling, which was meant to be irrevocable. His change of course was a new way of life (in contact with what then appeared to him to be better possibilities), in order to remain faithful to the deepest sense of his calling, when confronted with new needs. (According to Dominic's earliest biographers he could be moved to tears at the sight of the needs of others. Hence the desire of this realistic organizer—which remained with him all his life—to go to the Cumani, somewhere in the Balkans, evidently the place where the dualistic heresy crossed from East to West). The Order came into being from such an amazing change of course *in trust*. A change of course in trust is therefore part of the essence of the Dominican charisma.

No theologian, canon lawyer, professional psychologist or sociologist can work out at his study desk or in his armchair what we must do now. This must be tried by way of concrete experiment, by charismatically inspired religious, albeit bearing in mind the sometimes dangerously cross-grained element—the golden thread—in our Dominican family story. In so doing it will adopt, with due criticism, the successful attempts in the context of our past, gratefully rethinking them and making them fruitful in the context of the new programme. With Thomas Aquinas, who clearly followed the matter-of-fact and brilliant temperament of Dominic here, we can say, 'The excellence of a religious institution does not lie so much in the strictness of its observances as in the fact that these observances are designed with greater skill towards the purpose of the religious life.' And in the circumstances of our time this calls for a renewed and skilled religious decision in which all have a share, both high and low, so that the structures themselves remain open to this new cross-thread.

This question is our duty. For in our profession we also opt for a particular community, a Dominican community and its ideals. There can be such faults and defects in a particular community (whether through betrayal of the Dominican family story or because this story is no longer alive there and has become fossilized and dead) that *out of faithfulness* to his or her Dominican ideal the professed religious is ethically permitted (and in some cases may even be obliged) to leave the Dominican community because it does not give him or her the support to which they have a right by virtue of their profession. For paradoxically, here we expose ourselves to the danger that as Dominicans we may expel a 'Dominican charisma' from our ranks. The Dominican family story gives us adequate pointers if we also listen to God's voice in the characteristics of contemporary movements and trace their lines of force, so as to enrich this story with a new chapter which is still to be published. Many people think that the Dominican family story is exhausted, because hardly anyone still comes under its spell. Those of us who are Dominicans today, men and women, are the only ones who can give it a new twist so that the story flourishes again (not as a stunt or a sensation but as an authentic Dominican family story), so that others in turn will join the Dominican story-telling community and continue to hand the story on. Here we may also happily pass on the folklore which each order has along-side its own great story: that simply points to the fact that the great Dominican family story is made up of, and told by, ordinary, very human, people, though they transcend themselves through the strength of God's unmerited and loving grace. However, it would be fatal for the Dominican family story if this greater story eventually became narrower and was reduced to the story of the folklore of Dominican houses.

I am aware that I have said a great deal and very little. That is perhaps the most appropriate thing for the chapter which we are all adding, here and now, to the story of a great family tradition. I hope that it will become a serial which lasts longer than the stories which have entranced the whole world on television, but which have not in any way renewed the face of the earth: Neighbours, Coronation Street or the Forsyte Saga. May the Dominican story be a parable which in an unspoken, but compelling, way ends with the words of Jesus: 'Go and do likewise' (Luke 10.37).

In 1206, even before Dominic was thinking of a Dominican Order, he had founded a convent at Prouille. However, the aim of this convent was on the same lines: Dominic wanted to make the evangelical religious movement, which many women had also joined, into a church movement—that is, to bring the gospel to the church and to bring the church to sectarian gospel movements. Evangelism without the church or the church without evangelism is essentially un-Dominican, that is, it goes against the original charisma which brought the Order into being.

In Dominic's time, gospel inspiration was almost always to be found in 'deviant' movements. Hence Dominic's own preaching among the 'heretics.' From among such women (Waldensians who remained orthodox, the 'Catholic Poor') Dominic recruited the first occupants of Prouille: he gave a church atmosphere to the gospel they had experienced outside the church. In 1219 he also founded convents in Madrid and Rome (S. Sisto), to which he gave Constitutions (which would later also form the basis of the Dominican Order). After many difficulties the convent of S. Agnese was founded at Bologna with the financial support of an 18-year-old girl, Diana of Andalo (later the friend of the second General, Jordan of Saxony), but only after Dominic's death.

However, it is typical that at the end of his life Dominic, and after his death the whole male side of the Order, systematically began to oppose the incorporation of new convents into the Order. This opposition would involve them in fights with popes until 1259. It is evident from the archives that this opposition was motivated by the aim of the Order itself: the care of the sisters hindered the Dominicans in their task of preaching elsewhere. At a special Chapter in 1228 (in Paris) all Dominicans were prohibited from involvement in spiritual direction and pastoral care in our convents (with the exception of the first four great convents), on pain of expulsion from the Order. In northern areas, however, the growing Dominican movement had encountered the very lively evangelical women's movement there: all of a sudden this became Dominican (or sometimes Franciscan). After a time there were hundreds of convents, each with more than a hundred evangelical Dominican women. No one had planned this: it was a spontaneous consequence of the encounter between Dominican preaching and the evangelical women's movement of the time. After that, the male Dominicans came to be fundamentally opposed to having to care for the sisters, which hindered the purpose of their own Order. Time and again, papal bulls enjoined the Order against its will to provide both financial and spiritual care for these sisters. In 1252, at the Chapter of Bologna, the Order opposed the repeated papal bulls (occasioned by an appeal from our sisters to Rome). In a bull of 15 July 1252, Innocent IV made some concessions: Rome would stop issuing the bulls for the moment but the existing convents had to be taken into the care of the Dominicans.

However, the Dominicans would not accept this, and in the end they secured a retraction from the same pope, who said: 'I have allowed myself to be convinced that preaching is the most essential task of the Order. This aim must have priority and is hindered by the care of the women's convents. Therefore the pope resolves to release the Order from all obligations towards the convents . . . with the exceptions of Prouille and San Sisto in Rome.'

However, all the convents stormed the papal Curia with heartfelt pleas. The pope was caught between two Dominican fronts: the men and the women. He knew that the men were opposed in principle. Then the Master General, Jobannes Teutonicus, died (in 1252). Cardinal Hugo a Santo Caro, who had become a Dominican and was himself enthusiastic about the evangelical women's movement, was given full authority by the pope to come to an arrangement with the Order. First he wanted to break the opposition of the men 'with quiet measures': until the election of the new General (Humbert of Romans), the Dominicans had at least to take over the spiritual care of the sisters. The Order remained obstinate and at the Chapter of Milan in 1255 it was resolved that (in contrast to the monasteries) three successive General Chapters would be needed to come to a decision as to whether a convent was to come under Dominican direction. This first resolution was endorsed in Paris (1256) and Florence (1257) and thus became a Dominican ruling. In 1259 a definitive resolution was passed that all convents already established had the right to the pastoral care of Dominican priests. (This ending of resistance by the Order was the result of the mediation of the Dominican cardinal Hugo a Santo Caro, who combined both the official Dominican standpoint and that of the church in his own person. In the Order, from Dominic onwards, the specific Dominican character was often a compromise between the papal perspective and the views of the Dominicans; both parties knew how to secure the essentials of their position.) After about 30 years of opposition the Order capitulated: for new convents, the Dominican resolution, passed by three Chapters, remained in force. The combination of papal Curia and Dominican sisters had won the argument. Furthermore, the Order was obliged to make Constitutions for the whole of the women's side. In the General Chapter of 1259 at Valenciennes, Humbert of Romans approved the Dominican Constitutions as adapted for sisters. All this also gave the sisters economic security, so that they could devote themselves to a life of study and contemplation (since left to themselves, the sisters often lived in very real poverty—as a result of over-population). The close collaboration of male and female Dominicans that now took place resulted in the Dominican mystical movement which arose in the fourteenth century. This followed from the theological and mystical direction of women by Dominican lectors and the women's response to the direction (1300–1480). This was in the time of the Great Plague, which also affected thousands of Dominicans and had broken their initial verve. Furthermore, the Order was divided by the schism: Avignon and the two popes.

Later, above all in the nineteenth century, many congregations of sisters were founded outside the Order, so that the Order did not have any responsibility for them and no one was concerned for a truly Dominican spirituality: this spirit was often that of normal nineteenth-century religious life with its inspiration towards works of charity.

As Dominicans, therefore, we need to remember that in our day many developments have taken place in which men and women together are seeking a form of Dominican spirituality in a modern revival of life in accordance with the gospel, combined with social criticism. Although it is still a search, we may not simply rule out this Dominican possibility. A Dominican community spirit and the collaboration of Dominican brothers and sisters may perhaps help us to understand the mystical Dominican movement in the fourteenth century (a high point of Dominican spirituality). Taught by our own history, we may not dismiss possible new charismata out of hand. 'Dominican options' which are new and at first sight disconcerting are possibilities for the future and may not be suppressed *per se*, though we must pay attention to the danger of references to the religious past.

Timothy Radcliffe (1945–   )

Timothy Peter Joseph Radcliffe, 85th Master of the Order of Preachers, was born in London, England. His parents, Hugh Radcliffe and Maria Teresa Pereira, welcomed Timothy, their fourth son, on August 22, 1945. He entered the Order of Preachers and received the habit in 1965, made first vows one year later, and was solemnly professed in 1968. He was ordained a priest in Oxford in 1971. Speaking in Kentucky in 2003, he told the United States Conference of Major Superiors of Men that "the first tiny seed of my vocation was planted in my head by an ancient and eccentric Benedictine great uncle, and that was because he was one of the most joyful people I had ever met . . . . even as a child I could glimpse that this joy somehow came from that crazy way of life, which was poor, chaste and obedient."[1]

Timothy Radcliffe studied at Oxford and in Paris and received an M.A. from Oxford. He was chaplain to the University of London and Professor of New Testament, and was twice named Prior of the Convent of Blackfriars at Oxford. In April 1988, when he was forty-two, he was elected Provincial of the English Province of the Order of Preachers. He was elected Master of the Order four years later, at the 1992 General Elective Chapter in Mexico, and served from 1993 to 2001. He has preached at nuclear protests, spoken to learned societies, written books published in English, German, and French, and visited most of the countries in the world.

His academic interests revolve around the New Testament and sociology. He has said that he was "especially fascinated by the relationship between the theologies of the various authors of the New Testament, the forms in which they did theology (parables, letters, gospels, etc.)

---

1. Timothy Radcliffe, OP, "Religious Life in the World that is Coming to Be." Conference of Major Superiors of Men, CMSM National Assembly 2003, Louisville, Kentucky.

and the social transformation of the churches during the first century."[2] For many years he was involved in the promotion of justice and peace in England, where he also served as President of the National Conference of Religious. As Master of the Order he wrote and lectured widely on a variety of topics, all focused on the truth of the Gospel claim. His written works reflect his broad preparation in and his deep reflection on the issues of the day as reflected through the prism of Scripture.

Timothy Radcliffe is convinced of and dedicated to the truth. That truth exists or can be found and should be reverenced is a controversial concept that collides with postmodernity. As Radcliffe said when addressing SEDOS, the Service of Documentation and Studies on Mission headquartered in Rome:

> Here we encounter what is perhaps the deepest crisis in our mission today. There is a profound suspicion of anyone who claims to teach, unless they come from the East or have some strange New Age doctrine. Missionaries who teach are suspected of indoctrination, of cultural imperialism, of arrogance. Who are we to tell anyone what they should believe? To teach that Jesus is God is seen as indoctrination, whereas to teach that God is a sacred mushroom is part of the rich tapestry of human tradition! Anyway, our society is deeply skeptical of any truth claims. We live in Disneyland, in which the truth can be reinvented as we wish. In the virtual age, the truth is what you conjure up on your computer screen.[3]

For Timothy Radcliffe the truth is not conjured up, but exists as an object of study and belief. His entire life has been circumscribed by prayer, study, community, and dedication to the truth. The selection that follows is taken from an address he delivered at Yale University on October 8, 1996, as the invited Woodward Lecturer in the Department of Religious Studies.

Phyllis Zagano

---

2. Timothy Radcliffe, OP, "Talking to Strangers," 1996 Yale Woodward Lecture, October 8, 1996.

3. Timothy Radcliffe, OP, "Mission to a Runaway World: Future Citizens of the Kingdom," SEDOS 2000.

From *"Truth and Conflict"*

"Talking to Strangers," Address to Yale University, October 8, 1996

1996 Yale Woodward Lecturer
Department of Religious Studies

I am immensely honored to be asked to address you this afternoon. Although I have never been here before, I feel as if I were coming home. Most of my adult life I have been involved in universities, as a student, a chaplain, and finally as a teacher. I taught at Oxford for twelve years, first as a member of Blackfriars, the Dominican house of studies, and then also as a member of the theology faculty. One could say that I am a jack of all trades and master of the Dominican Order. My main interest was in the field of New Testament studies and sociology. I was especially fascinated by the relationship between the theologies of the various authors of the New Testament, the forms in which they did theology (parables, letters, gospels etc.) and the social transformation of the churches during the first century.

***

Eight years ago, this happy academic life, giving tutorials and lectures and sometimes sleeping in the Bodleian Library, was brought to an abrupt end. After a few years as Provincial of England, I moved to Rome. It meant substituting airports for libraries. In my first three years as Master of the Order I visited 83 countries. I was confronted with a world whose violence and poverty I had never imagined. I discovered that for very many of my brothers and sisters, being a member of a religious Order today meant living dangerously.

I shall never forget a trip to Rwanda, when the country was beginning to erupt. After a day of being confronted with so much violence, so much misery, we were reduced to silence. There was nothing to say. Thanks be to God, literally, we were given something to do, the ritual of the Eucharist, a rite to express what we could not articulate. And then there were visits to Algeria, where our brothers and sisters live in daily danger of death. Two months ago I stayed with brothers who work in the Amazon, who receive regular death threats from the local landowners who openly admit that they liquidate anyone who opposes them, sometimes boiling their bodies and feeding them to the pigs. And when I met a group of brothers and sisters recently from the States, and asked them what they believed to be the principal challenge for us in America today, they too claimed that it was violence.

Two very different lives then. It would be easy to suggest that after years of living in the ivory tower of the university I had at last met the world as it was, "the real world" as some say. My reaction is different though. I have become more than ever convinced of the importance of institutions such as Yale or Oxford for the future of our society. We have a need of such places of reflection and research if we are to heal our society of its violence and rebuild the human community. This afternoon I wish to share with you a few simple convictions as to why this is so, and what we should hope for from such centres of study. I am very aware that in doing so I shall raise complex philosophical issues which I am unqualified to answer. But that is where I hope that you will help me.

1. Beyond the "Single Vision"

If you will forgive me an enormous oversimplification, then I would suggest that one root of this social crisis, and there are others, is what might be termed a crisis of truth. I wonder whether there has ever been such a violent century, beginning with the First World War, and its millions of dead, the death camps of Auschwitz and Dachau, the bombs of Hiroshima and Nagasaki, and the endless hemorrhaging of human society since then in war, and poverty and starvation. There are many reasons for this, from the globalization of the economy to the development of technology. Yet one seed of this violence is surely that we have lost confidence in our ability to seek the truth together, and so to build a common human home in which we may recognize ourselves and each other.

***

Whenever I set off on a trip, the hardest decision is as to what books to take with me. What can I read in the planes and waiting in the airports to save me from brain death? And so for my last trip, already becoming a bit nervous about having accepted to address you, I decided to take Newman's *The Idea of a University*. His definition of the purpose of a university will probably seem vastly over optimistic to us. The university exists, he writes, to educate "the intellect to reason well in all matters, to reach out towards truth and to grasp it." There is a wonderful Victorian confidence about that statement: "to reach out towards truth and to grasp it." It may smack of intellectual arrogance to us.

Yet what I found fascinating was Newman's description of how the university trains us to reach out for the truth. He wrote, "We know, not by a direct and simple vision, not at a glance, but, as it were, by piecemeal and accumulation, by a mental process, by going round an object, by the comparison, the combination, the mutual correction, the continual adaptation of many partial no-tions, by the employment, concentration, and joint action of many faculties and exercises of mind."

The process of seeking the truth, then, is not for Newman through the direct and univocal perception of some single vision, but a much more tentative, fumbling, humble approach, trying to feel one's way through "many partial notions." This is evocative of what has been my own experience in trying to understand scriptural texts. You cannot march in and claim their meaning with the aid of some grand theory. Study is much more like sneak-ing up on the meaning of the text, trying this approach and then another, inching one's way towards understanding. You may begin with a historico-critical approach and then a moment comes when you feel that this is not yielding anything more, and you try to slide up on the text from a sociological perspective; then maybe the time has come from a bit of literary analysis. To take an image from Wittgenstein, you must be like a carpenter who knows when to use each tool in the bag; when to use a hammer and when a chisel; when you need glue or when to use a screwdriver.

Emily Dickenson describes well how one has to slink up on the truth, aslant, rather than grabbing it by the forelocks:

> Tell all the Truth but tell it slant
> Success in circuit lies
> Too bright for our infirm delight
> The Truth's superb surprise
> As lightning to the children eased
> With explanation kind
> The Truth must dazzle gradually
> Or ever man be blind.

Creeping up on the truth of a text, or a person, or anything else, is always a matter of letting oneself be thrown by "The Truth's superb surprise." It is letting oneself be astonished, discovering that one did not know in advance what was to be discovered.

Our society is marked by a deep distrust of all teachers. Nicholas Lash, from Cambridge, wrote (in the book that I took on my last trip to Burundi): "The Enlightenment left us with what we might call a crisis of docility. Unless we have the courage to work things out for ourselves, to take as true only that which we have personally attained or, perhaps invented, then meanings and values, descriptions and instructions, imposed by other people, feeding other people's power, will inhibit and enslave us, bind us into fables and falsehoods from the past. Even God's truth, perhaps especially God's truth, is no exception to this rule. Only slaves and children should be teachable, or docile."

Perhaps the first requirement of a good university teacher is that he or she refuses to be a guru, to be the one who knows. St. Thomas Aquinas, (and as a good Dominican I must mention him at least once a lecture) strongly maintained that no one can, strictly speaking, teach anyone anything. The Angelic Doctor loved to quote the "no one your Master." All that the teacher can do is to accompany the students in their process of discovery.

So, in an age of agnosticism and ayatollahs, the role of the university is to be the place where we learn that the truth may be sought. It is not to be captured with the cleanness of a single vision, but sneaked up on, through many partial notions, many inadequate theories, through all sorts of tools, and it comes to us finally as a surprise and a gift. In that sense, it is the paradoxical role of the University teacher to introduce us into the humility of learning. Not because we must learn to submit to a teacher, but because the teacher shows him or herself to be someone just on the way, the doctor as fellow disciple. Jordan of Saxony, Dominic's successor as Master of the Order, said of Dominic that he understood everything *"humili cordis intelligentia,"* through the humble intelligence of his heart.

I am not suggesting that universities are the only places in which we may be initiated into this truth seeking. Families, monasteries, women's groups, guilds, religious orders, schools of artists, all these should be places of learning too. But since the thirteenth century, the university has been a central place for keeping alive this hunger for truth.

***

2. Talking with the Stranger

So far, I have taken a first step or arguing for the importance of universities as places of resistance to the imperialism of the single vision. The university teacher should induct us into the necessary tentativeness, hesitancy, and even humility which is central to our approach to truth. We need a multiplicity of crafts and skills, lots of tools in our bag, and not the pretensions of one big sledge hammer of a theory.

Now I would like to explore another aspect, which is that universities should be places where we learn to talk to strangers. Before I wrote these lines, in a week in Rome snatched between trips to Brazil and to Spain, I heard the announcement of the *coup d'état* in Burundi, and I have just heard some news of a bomb in Atlanta. A consequence of the conflicting fundamentalisms of our time, is that those who are different easily become not just strangers but enemies with whom it is impossible to talk. Simone Weil wrote, *"Tuer tous les hommes qui ne pensent pas comme moi. A la limite on reste seul. Imitation de la solitude de Dieu; c'est là la pire idolâtrie."*

How can we learn to talk to strangers? What conversation can we initiate with those who are different? And what role can the university play in preparing us for this dialogue?

The most dramatic experience that I have had of the pain of dialogue was indeed in Burundi some two years ago. It was during the first explosion of violence, which killed perhaps as many as a hundred thousand people. That would be as if 4 million people were killed in the USA. It was the old conflict between Cain and Abel, between the semi-nomadic Tutsis with their cattle, and the peasant farmers who are Hutus. Our brothers in Burundi come from both ethnic groups, and all had lost brothers and sisters and family. The struggle was to witness to the gospel by somewhere staying together. I visited the country with the local superior, a Tutsi, and a member of the General Council of the Order, who is a Hutu. Before I left we gathered everyone together to celebrate the Eucharist, the sacrament of unity. But what could we all say to each other? As in Rwanda, what was most important was what we could do, repeating the gestures performed by a man in the face of his betrayal and death. Each brother could and did talk of his suffering, of those who he had lost, so that they were joined in the suffering rather than divided by it.

One of the functions of the Church, and of a religious Order, is to try to be present in those places of deafness and incomprehension, to offer a space where conversations may begin. I think of an ecumenical community I visited in Belfast, which was literally on the frontier between the tribal lands of Catholics and Protestants. It was a place where quietly, slowly, a few brave souls could try to knit some common language. It was above all the women who had the courage to do this. One of our Dominican brothers, Pierre Claverie, was the bishop of Oran in Algeria. He was assassinated by a bomb two months ago. Shortly before his death he wrote:

> "The Church accomplishes its vocation and its mission when she is present in the ruptures which crucify humanity in its flesh and its unity. Jesus is dead spread-eagled between heaven and earth, arms stretched out to gather together the children of God dispersed by the sin which separates them, isolates them and sets them over against each other and against God himself. God has placed himself on the lines of fracture born of this sin. In Algeria, we are on one of these seismic lines which divide the world: Islam/The West, North/South, rich/poor. We are truly in our place, because it is here that one may glimpse the light of the Resurrection."

But how in these hard places can we learn to talk to strangers? I wish to suggest the university should be one of the places in which we learn to talk to those who are different. Steiner wrote, "Apprehension (the meeting with the other) signifies both fear and perception." The meeting of the other is a fearful moment, but it can become a moment of recognition, of understanding. Thinking can open my eyes to see the stranger and build the common human home.

Part of our apprenticeship is surely in learning to read texts written by strangers, and come to understand them. Struggling with St. Paul or Augustine, with Descartes or the texts of the French Revolution, requires of one an openness to the other. It is not unlike an education in friendship. Lash argues this strongly:

> "Good learning calls, no less than teaching does, for courtesy, respect, a kind of reverence: for facts and people, evidence and argument, for climates of speech and patterns of behaviour different from our own. Watchfulness is, indeed, in order, but endless suspicion and mistrust are not. There are affinities between the courtesy, the delicacy of attentiveness, required for friendship; the single-minded passionate disinterestedness with which no good scholarly work can be done; and the contemplativity which strains, without credulity, to listen for the voice of God—who does not shout."

Nicholas Lash spoke of "the single-minded passionate disinterest-edness without which no good scholarly work can be done." This word "disinterestedness" is worth pausing over. It suggests how the university should be the locus of an alternative perception of reality.

But in what sense does scholarly work offer a disinterested perception of things. It would be easy and wrong to mistake this for a distance, a disengagement from concern and commitment. That would be the "lack of conviction" of the best. And it is surely a temptation of the academic world to fall into a sort of critical de-tachment which frees our hearts from risks of engagement and commitment, in the name of intellectual freedom. Faced with our messy violent world we may claim a scholarly detachment which justifies keeping one's hands clean. When D. H. Lawrence went to Cambridge and met the group of philosophers gathered around Russell he was shocked:

> "What does Russell really want? (he asked) He wants to keep his own established ego, his finite and ready defined self intact, free from contact and connection. He wants to be ultimately a free agent. That is what they all want, ultimately . . . so that in their own souls they can be independent little gods, referred nowhere and to nothing, little mortal Absolutes, secure from question."

Regardless of whether it is just or not, and one could hardly call Russell uncommitted, it offers a wonderful image of the wrong sort of disinterestedness. There can be a detachment which insu-lates and protects, an academic carapace which makes one invul-nerable and apart.

I suspect that the disinterestedness that Lash has in mind is quite other. It is a refusal to let one's perception of anything be dominated by an "interest." This is the temptation of any single vision. The Khmer Rouge did not see its prisoners as individuals, but were interested in them merely as functions of the wheel of history, actors in the great class struggle. The consumer society will not delight in the cow for its own sake, but see it as potential profit, unless it happens to be a sad mad English cow. In this cul-ture of greed, then perhaps study requires of us a certain way of life, a certain freedom from acquisitiveness. We may have to learn to see things with unpossessive eyes. It is no coincidence that when Dominic founded an Order dedicated to study, he made poverty central to our way of life. I am not suggesting that all faculty members at Yale should take a vow of poverty though I would be happy to talk to anyone over drinks who wants to join the Order. The disinterestedness of the scholar is not the detachment of someone who holds back. It is more like the disinterestedness of friendship.

So learning to study the texts of strangers is part of my human formation, and forms me as someone who is capable of relating to another: another time, another view, another person. The Constitutions of my Order speak of study as *"hominum propensinem ad veritatem excollant,"* "the cultivation of humanity's natural inclination to the truth." This *propensio ad veritatem*, the inclination to truth that we need to cultivate, is not just a human desire to know many things, but a natural human desire to reach out to those who are different, to break the tight hold of our egocentricity, a solipsistic self-obsession. It wakens us from the illusion that we are the centre of the world. Whether we are studying the ending of Mark's gospel or the sexual habits of a rare snail, our eyes are being opened to see what is other. Study is ecstatic.

I would even go so far as to say that study can touch and heal the deepest hunger of the human being, which is to love. The perception of the other belongs to loving them. As Simone Weil wrote, *"On ne reconnait pleinement l'existence que de ceux que l ' on aime."*

For example, Augustine's conversion to Christianity was both a falling in love and a moment of understanding. It was an intellectual act and a transformation of his heart:

> "Late have I loved you, O beauty so ancient and so new; late have I loved you. . . . I tasted you and I now hunger and thirst for you; you touched me and I have burnt for your peace."

***

But if universities are to train us in the delicate art of talking to strangers, then it is not enough that we struggle with texts and try to understand the dead. Ultimately a university will contribute to the building of human community and to the art of dialogue if we are able to talk with each other. Newman once wrote that if he had to choose between a university with highly trained professors, rigorous examinations and which taught the pupils lots of facts, or one in which a lot of young people merely met and debated with each other, then he would without hesitation choose the latter. Because the primary function of a University is to teach us to be social beings, able to talk, to listen and learn from those who are different.

This is a wonderful idea. Yet in my experience this can be hard. Even here, where we are all supposed to be rational and intelligent, dialogue can be hard. How far are we able to argue with our colleagues, and seek the truth together? How open are we to having our favourite theories questioned? Perhaps the greatest challenge that universities face, if they are to contribute to the healing of our bruised world, is to learn that pleasure of debate with those who are different.

***

When I was a young Dominican student we still sometimes practised a version of the medieval *disputatio*. This was a form of debating central to the life of the thirteenth century university, and it embodies a vision of what a university should be about. It does not seem to have been practised often by the Inquisition, but it represents an ideal which has something to offer us. In the *disputatio* the aim was not so much to demonstrate that your opponent was utterly and in every way wrong, and to be derided and dismissed as a fool. Instead you had to show the limited sense in which he was right. If someone were to assert that "Yale Department of Religious Studies is better than the Theology Faculty of Oxford," I might reply in making a distinction: "That Yale is better as far as sociological analysis I accept; that it is better in every way I deny." The aim was, through disagreement and mutual criticism, to arrive at a common truth, that was able to accommodate what was true in each position.

Perhaps even in universities we have been seduced by a competitive form of debate, which is as blind and violent as the struggle of the species to survive in the Darwinian jungle, or as senseless as the struggle for mastery between Coca Cola and Pepsi Cola. But we are called to be a place of counter-culture, of a different way of relating, through which one believes that one may learn something from those with whom one disagrees. This requires of us compassion and vulnerability. Iris Murdock said that when we disagree with someone else, we must ask of what they are afraid. How can we enter their perception of things, and rescue what is right and true from what is wrong and misguided?

I wish to conclude by reading to you a poem by Czeslaw Milosz, in praise of reason "beautiful and invincible." It captures something of the vocation of the university. And this reason that it praises is surely not that arrogant reason of the single vision, which believes that it can grasp the truth with an unhesitating clarity and arrogance, but that more humble reason which arrives at a just perception hesitantly, through many "partial notions," using all the tools she can find, delighting in debate and dialogue:

> Human reason is beautiful and invincible.
> No bars, no barbed wire, no pulping of books,
> No sentence of banishment can prevail against it.
> It establishes the universal ideas in language,
> And guides our hand so we write Truth and Justice
> With capital letters, lie and oppression with small.
> It puts what should be above things as they are,
> Is an enemy of despair and a friend of hope.
> It does not know Jew from Greek, or slave from master,
> Giving us the estate of the world to manage.
> It saves austere and transparent phrases
> From the filthy discord of tortured words.
> It says that everything is new under the sun,
> Opens the congealed fist of the past.
> Beautiful and very young are Philo-Sophia
> And poetry, her ally in the service of the good.
> As late as yesterday Nature celebrated their birth,
> The News was brought to the mountains by a unicorn
> and an echo.
> Their friendship will be glorious, their time has no limit.
> Their enemies have delivered themselves to destruction.

Afterword

Until the Friars' 1974 General Chapter held at Madonna dell'Arco, near Naples, Italy, the traditional demarcation of the branches of the Dominican Order were the First Order (priests, deacons, brothers), Second Order (nuns), and Third Order (lay Dominican tertiaries), all bound to the Master General by vows, and the Third Order Regular (apostolic sisters), not so bound. The Dominican Youth Movement, Dominican secular institutes, and lay associates of sisters' congregations have since enlarged the Dominican Family:

> The Dominican Family, then, consists of friars, nuns, sisters of apostolic life, members of secular institutes, priestly fraternities and laity who belong to fraternities or new groups accepted by the Order. . . . Thus, as if arising from a tree planted beside living fountains, the branches of the Dominican Family are numerous. Each one has its own character, its special status, its autonomy. However, since all participate in the charism of Saint Dominic, they share the very same vocation to be preachers in the Church.

Acts of the General Chapter of Friars (Mexico, 1992)

Recent statistics count 6,000 friars (1,000 in studies) in 600 convents and houses worldwide; 4,000 nuns in 234 monasteries; and 29,000 sisters (800 in studies) in 160 congregations as well as 70,000 members of Dominican lay fraternities and secular institutes around the world.

Dominicans follow the Rule of Saint Augustine. While several documents have been identified as Augustine's Rule, including his Letter 211 addressed to a community of women; his Sermons 355 and 356 entitled "De vitâ et moribus clericorum suorum"; a portion of the Rule drawn up for clerks or *Consortia monachorum*; a Rule known as *Regula secunda*; and another Rule called: "De vitâ eremiticâ ad sororem liber," Letter 211 and Sermons 355 and 356 are certain to have been written by Augustine.

Letter 211 is among the influences on Benedict in the creation of his Rule. This letter was part of a collection of "Rules of the Fathers" and influenced the writings of other monastic founders. When community life was directed for secular clergy in the 11th century, it was organized according to Letter 211 and Sermons 355 and 356. Similarly, early communities of canons and canonesses used Letter 211 as their guiding document. What is now known as the Rule of Saint Augustine became the Rule of the Premonstratensians and of Canons Regular and was adopted by Dominic for the Friars of the Order of Preachers.

In addition to the Rule of Saint Augustine, Dominicans have Constitutions, which interpret the Rule and govern particularly. Neither these nor the Rule bind under pain of sin, a point Dominic insisted upon in order to free his followers to follow the core of their vocations, particularly apostolic preaching. The primitive Constitutions framed during Dominic's present the framework of conventual life, government of the Order, and its apostolate. In essence, the Constitutions present the reflective sides of Dominican life: love of God and of neighbor, each flowing one from the other. Prayer in its prescribed forms engages the soul and sends it forth to serve the other, and such service in God's name draws the Dominican back to formal public liturgy and the private or "secret" prayer that complements it.

While the Constitutions of the Order, of the nuns, and of various congregations of sisters differ in detail, each flows from and forms a commentary to the Rule of Saint Augustine.

Phyllis Zagano

The Rule of Saint Augustine

Chapter One

Purpose and Basis of Common Life

Before all else, dear brothers, love God and then your neighbor, because these are the chief commandments given to us.

1. The following are the precepts we order you living in the monastery to observe.

2. The main purpose for you having come together is to live harmoniously in your house, intent upon God in oneness of mind and heart.

3. Call nothing your own, but let everything be yours in common. Food and clothing shall be distributed to each of you by your superior, not equally to all, for all do not enjoy equal health, but rather according to each one's need. For so you read in the Acts of the Apostles that they had all things in common and distribution was made to each one according to each one's need (4:32, 35).

4. Those who owned something in the world should be careful in wanting to share it in common once they have entered the monastery.

5. But they who owned nothing should not look for those things in the monastery that they were unable to have in the world. Nevertheless, they are to be given all that their health requires even if, during their time in the world, poverty made it impossible for them to find the very necessities of life. And those should not consider themselves fortunate because they have found the kind of food and clothing which they were unable to find in the world.

6. And let them not hold their heads high because they associate with people whom they did not dare to approach in the world, but let them rather lift up their hearts and not seek after what is vain and earthly. Otherwise monasteries will come to serve a useful purpose for the rich and not the poor, if the rich are made humble there and the poor are puffed up with pride.

7. The rich, for their part, who seemed important in the world, must not look down upon their brothers who have come into this holy brotherhood from a condition of poverty. They should seek to glory in the fellowship of poor brothers rather than in the reputation of rich relatives. They should neither be elated if they have contributed a part of their wealth to the common life, nor take more pride in sharing their riches with the monastery than if they were to enjoy them in the world. Indeed, every other kind of sin has to do with the commission of evil deeds, whereas pride lurks even in good works in order to destroy them. And what good is it to scatter one's wealth abroad by giving to the poor, even to become poor oneself, when the unhappy soul is thereby more given to pride in despising riches than it had been in possessing them?

8. Let all of you then live together in oneness of mind and heart, mutually honoring God in yourselves, whose temples you have become.

Chapter Two

Prayer

1. Be assiduous in prayer (Col 4:2), at the hours and times appointed.

2. In the Oratory no one should do anything other than that for which it was intended and from which it also takes its name. Consequently, if there are some who might wish to pray there during their free time, even outside the hours appointed, they should not be hindered by those who think something else must be done there.

3. When you pray to God in psalms and hymns, think over in your hearts the words that come from your lips.

4. Chant only what is prescribed for chant; moreover, let nothing be chanted unless it is so prescribed.

Chapter Three

Moderation and Self-Denial

1. Subdue the flesh, so far as your health permits, by fasting and abstinence from food and drink. However, when someone is unable to fast, he should still take no food outside mealtimes unless he is ill.

2. When you come to table, listen until you leave to what is the custom to read, without disturbance or strife. Let not your mouths alone take nourishment but let your hearts too hunger for the words of God.

3. If those in more delicate health from their former way of life are treated differently in the matter of food, this should not be a source of annoyance to the others or appear unjust in the eyes of those who owe their stronger health to different habits of life. Nor should the healthier brothers deem them more fortunate for having food which they do not have, but rather consider themselves fortunate for having the good health which the others do not enjoy.

4. And if something in the way of food, clothing, and bedding is given to those coming to the monastery from a more genteel way of life, which is not given to those who are stronger, and therefore happier, then these latter ought to consider how far these others have come in passing from their life in the world down to this life of ours, though they have been unable to reach the level of frugality common to the stronger brothers. Nor should all want to receive what they see given in larger measure to the few, not as a token of honor, but as a help to support them in their weakness. This would give rise to a deplorable disorder—that in the monastery, where the rich are coming to bear as much hardship as they can, the poor are turning to a more genteel way of life.

5. And just as the sick must take less food to avoid discomfort, so too, after their illness, they are to receive the kind of treatment that will quickly restore their strength, even though they come from a life of extreme poverty. Their more recent illness has, as it were, afforded them what accrued to the rich as part of their former way of life. But when they have recovered their former strength they should go back to their happier way of life which, because their needs are fewer, is all the more in keeping with God's servants. Once in good health they must not become slaves to the enjoyment of food which was necessary to sustain them in their illness. For it is better to suffer a little want than to have too much.

Chapter Four

Safeguarding Chastity, and Fraternal Correction

1. There should be nothing about your clothing to attract attention. Besides, you should not seek to please by your apparel, but by a good life.

2. Whenever you go out, walk together, and when you reach your destination, stay together.

3. In your walk, deportment, and in all actions, let nothing occur to give offense to anyone who sees you, but only what becomes your holy state of life.

4. Although your eyes may chance to rest upon some woman or other, you must not fix your gaze upon any woman. Seeing women when you go out is not forbidden, but it is sinful to desire them or to wish them to desire you, for it is not by tough or passionate feeling alone but by one's gaze also that lustful desires mutually arise. And do not say that your hearts are pure if there is immodesty of the eye, because the unchaste eye carries the message of an impure heart. And when such hearts disclose their unchaste desires in a mutual gaze, even without saying a word, then it is that chastity suddenly goes out of their life, even though their bodies remain unsullied by unchaste acts.

5. And whoever fixes his gaze upon a woman and likes to have hers fixed upon him must not suppose that others do not see what he is doing. He is very much seen, even by those he thinks do not see him. But suppose all this escapes the notice of man—what will he do about God who sees from on high and from whom nothing is hidden? Or are we to imagine that he does not see because he sees with a patience as great as his wisdom? Let the religious man then have such fear of God that he will not want to be an occasion of sinful pleasure to a woman. Ever mindful that God sees all things, let him not desire to look at a woman lustfully. For it is on this point that fear of the Lord is recommended, where it is written: An abomination to the Lord is he who fixes his gaze (Prov 27:20).

6. So when you are together in church and anywhere else where women are present, exercise a mutual care over purity of life. Thus by mutual vigilance over one another will God, who dwells in you, grant you his protection.

7. If you notice in someone of your brothers this wantonness of the eye of which I am speaking, admonish him at once so that the beginning of evil will not grow more serious but will be promptly corrected.

8. But if you see him doing the same thing again on some other day, even after your admonition, then whoever had occasion to discover this must report him as he would a wounded man in need of treatment. But let the offense first be pointed out to two or three so that he can be proven guilty on the testimony of these two or three and be punished with due severity. And do not charge yourselves with ill will when you bring this offense to light. Indeed, yours is the greater blame if you allow your brothers to be lost through your silence when you are able to bring about their correction by your disclosure. If your brother, for example, were suffering a bodily wound that he wanted to hide for fear of undergoing treatment, would it not be cruel of you to remain silent and a mercy on your part to make this known? How much greater then is your obligation to make his condition known lest he continue to suffer a more deadly wound of the soul.

9. But if he fails to correct the fault despite this admonition, he should first be brought to the attention of the superior before the offense is made known to the others who will have to prove his guilt, in the event he denies the charge. Thus, corrected in private, his fault can perhaps be kept from the others. But should he feign ignorance, the others are to be summoned so that in the presence of all he can be proven guilty, rather than stand accused on the word of one alone. Once proven guilty, he must undergo salutary punishment according to the judgment of the superior or priest having the proper authority. If he refuses to submit to punishment he shall be expelled from your brotherhood even if he does not withdraw of his own accord. For this too is not done out of cruelty, but from a sense of compassion so that many others may not be lost through his bad example.

10. And let everything I have said about not fixing one's gaze be also observed carefully and faithfully with regard to other offenses: to find them out, to ward them off, to make them known, to prove and punish them—all out of love for man and a hatred of sin.

11. But if anyone should go so far in wrongdoing as to receive letters in secret from any woman, or small gifts of any kind, you ought to show mercy and pray for him if he confesses this of his own accord. But if the offense is detected and he is found guilty, he must be more severely chastised according to the judgment of the priest or superior.

Chapter Five

The Care of Community Goods and Treatment of the Sick

1. Keep your clothing in one place in charge of one or two, or of as many as are needed to care for them and to prevent damage from moths. And just as you have your food from the one pantry, so, too, you are to receive your clothing from a single wardrobe. If possible, do not be concerned about what you are given to wear at the change of seasons, whether each of you gets back what he had put away or something different, providing no one is denied what he needs. If, however, disputes and murmuring arise on this account because someone complains that he received poorer clothing than he had before, and thinks it is beneath him to wear the kind of clothing worn by another, you may judge from this how lacking you are in that holy and inner garment of the heart when you quarrel over garments for the body. But if allowance is made for your weakness and you do receive the same clothing you had put away, you must still keep it in one place under the common charge.

2. In this way no one shall perform any task for his own benefit, but all your work shall be done for the common good, with greater zeal and more dispatch than if each one of you were to work for yourself alone. For charity, as it is written, is not self-seeking (1 Cor 13:5), meaning that it places the common good before its own, not its own before the common good. So whenever you show greater concern for the common good than for your own, you may know that you are growing in charity. Thus let the abiding virtue of charity prevail in all things that minister to the fleeting necessities of life.

3. It follows, therefore, that if anyone brings something for their sons or other relatives living in the monastery, whether a garment or anything else they think is needed, this must not be accepted secretly as one's own but must be placed at the disposal of the superior so that, as common property, it can be given to whoever needs it. But if someone secretly keeps something given to him, he shall be judged guilty of theft.

4. Your clothing should be cleaned either by yourselves or by those who perform this service, as the superior shall determine, so that too great a desire for clean clothing may not be the source of interior stains on the soul.

5. As for bodily cleanliness too, a brother must never deny himself the use of the bath when his health requires it. But this should be done

on medical advice, without complaining, so that even though unwilling, he shall do what has to be done for his health when the superior orders it. However, if the brother wishes it when it might not be good for him, you must not comply with his desire, for sometimes we think something is beneficial for the pleasure it gives, even though it may prove harmful.

6. Finally, if the cause of a brother's bodily pain is not apparent, you may take the word of God's servant when he indicates what is giving him pain. But if it remains uncertain whether the remedy he likes is good for him, a doctor should be consulted.

7. When there is need to frequent the public baths or any other place, no fewer than two or three should go together, and whoever has to go somewhere must not go with those of his own choice but with those designated by the superior.

8. The care of the sick, whether those in convalescence or others suffering from some indisposition, even though free of fever, shall be assigned to a brother who can personally obtain from the pantry whatever he sees is necessary for each one.

9. Those in charge of the pantry, or of clothing and books, should render cheerful service to their brothers.

10. Books are to be requested at a fixed hour each day, and anyone coming outside that hour is not to receive them.

11. But as for clothing and shoes, those in charge shall not delay the giving of them whenever they are required by those in need of them.

Chapter Six

Asking Pardon and Forgiving Offenses

1.You should either avoid quarrels altogether or else put an end to them as quickly as possible; otherwise anger may grow into hatred, making a plank out of a splinter, and turn the soul into a murderer. For so you read: Everyone who hates his brother is a murderer (1 John 3:15).

2. Whoever has injured another by open insult, or by abusive or even incriminating language, must remember to repair the injury as quickly as possible by an apology, and he who suffered the injury must also forgive, without further wrangling. But if they have offended one another they must forgive one another's trespasses for the sake of your prayers, which should be recited with greater sincerity each time you repeat them. Although a brother is often tempted to anger, yet prompt to ask pardon from one he admits to having offended, such a one is

better than another who, though less given to anger, finds it too hard to ask forgiveness. But a brother who is never willing to ask pardon, or does not do so from his heart, has no reason to be in the monastery, even if he is not expelled. You must then avoid being too harsh in your words, and should they escape your lips, let those same lips not be ashamed to heal the wounds they have caused.

3. But whenever the good of discipline requires you to speak harshly in correcting your subjects, then, even if you think you have been unduly harsh in your language, you are not required to ask forgiveness lest, by practicing too great humility toward those who should be your subjects, the authority to rule is undermined. But you should still ask forgiveness from the Lord of all, who knows with what deep affection you love even those whom you might happen to correct with undue severity. Besides, you are to love another with a spiritual rather than an earthly love.

Chapter Seven

Governance and Obedience

1. The superior should be obeyed as a father with the respect due him, so as not to offend God in his person, and, even more so, the priest who bears responsibility for you all.

2. But it shall pertain chiefly to the superior to see that these precepts are all observed and, if any point has been neglected, to take care that the transgression is not carelessly overlooked but is punished and corrected. In doing so he must refer whatever exceeds the limit and power of his office to the priest who enjoys greater authority among you.

3. The superior, for his part, must not think himself fortunate in his exercise of authority but in his role as one serving you in love. In your eyes he shall hold the first place among you by the dignity of his office, but in fear before God he shall be as the least among you. He must show himself as an example of good works toward all. Let him admonish the unruly, cheer the fainthearted, support the weak, and be patient toward all (1 Thess 5:14). Let him uphold discipline while instilling fear. And though both are necessary, he should strive to be loved by you rather than feared, ever mindful that he must give an account of you to God.

4. It is by being more obedient, therefore, that you show mercy not only toward yourselves but also toward the superior whose higher rank among you exposes him all the more to greater peril.

Chapter Eight

Observance of the Rule

1. The Lord grant that you may observe all these precepts in a spirit of charity as lovers of spiritual beauty, giving forth the good odor of Christ in the holiness of your lives: not as slaves living under the law but as men living in freedom under grace.

2. And that you may see yourselves in this little book, as in a mirror, have it read to you once a week so as to neglect no point through forgetfulness. When you find that you are doing all that has been written, give thanks to the Lord, the Giver of every good. But when one of you finds that he has failed on any point, let him be sorry for the past, be on his guard for the future, praying that he will be forgiven his fault and not be led into temptation.

Bibliography

The Dominican Tradition

Ashley, Benedict M., O.P. *The Dominicans*. Collegeville: Liturgical Press, 1990.

Borgman, Eric. *Dominican Spirituality*, tr. John Bowden. New York: Continuum, 2000.

Coffey, Reginald M., O.P. *The American Dominicans: A History of St. Joseph's Province*. Washington, DC: Mt. Vernon Publishing Company, 1970.

Hinnebusch, William A., O.P. *The Dominicans: A Short History*. New York: Alba House, 1975.

_____. *Dominican Spirituality: Principles and Practice*. Washington, DC: Dominicana Publications, 1964.

_____. *The History of the Dominican Order: Origins and Growth to 1500*. Vol. 1. New York: Alba House, 1966.

_____. *The History of the Dominican Order: Intellectual and Cultural Life to 1500*. Vol. 2. New York: Alba House, 1973.

The Book of Constitutions and Ordinations of the Brothers of the Order of Preachers. Timothy Radcliffe (Corporate Author: Dominicans) Dublin, 2001.

The Rule of Saint Augustine: Masculine and Feminine Versions, tr. Raymond Canning, O.S.A. London: Darton, Longman and Todd; Kalamazoo, MI: Cistercian Publications, 1984, 1996.

Dominic de Guzmán (1170–1221)

Jarrett, Bede, O.P. *Life of St. Dominic*. Westminister, MD: Newman Press, 1955.

Lehner, Francis C., O.P. *Saint Dominic: Biographical Documents*. Washington, DC: The Thomist Press, 1964.

Vicaire, M. H., O.P. *Saint Dominic and His Times*, tr. Kathleen Pond. New York: McGraw-Hill, 1964.

138

Albert the Great (1207–1280)

Albert and Thomas: Selected Writings, tr. Simon Tugwell, O.P. The Classics of Western Spirituality. New York: Paulist, 1988.

The book of secrets of Albertus Magnus of the virtues of herbs, stones and certain beasts, also A book of the marvels of the world, tr. Michael R. Best, Michael and Frank Brightman. Oxford: Clarendon Press, 1973.

Book of minerals, tr. Dorothy Wyckoff. Oxford: Clarendon Press, 1967.

Man and the beasts (De animalibus, books 22–26), tr. James J. Scanlan. Binghamton, NY: Medieval & Renaissance Texts & Studies, 1987.

Libellus de alchimia, ascribed to Albertus Magnus, tr. Virginia Heines. Berkeley: University of California Press, 1958.

On animals: a medieval summa zoologica, tr. Kenneth Kitchell and I. M. Resnick. Baltimore: Johns Hopkins University Press, 1999.

Libellus de natura animalium, tr. John I. Davis. London: Dawson's of Pall Mall, 1958.

Schwertner, Thomas M. *Saint Albert the Great.* Milwaukee: Bruce, 1932.

Supplement to the Liturgy of the Hours for the Order of Preachers: A Draft Translation of the Proprium Officiorum Ordinis Praedicatorum (1982) for Study and Consultation. River Forest, IL: Dominican Liturgical Commission, U.S.A., 1991.

Weisheipl, James A., O.P., ed. *Albertus Magnus and the Sciences.* Toronto: Pontifical Institute of Medieval Studies, 1980.

Thomas Aquinas (1225–1274)

Albert and Thomas: Selected Writings, tr. Simon Tugwell, O.P. The Classics of Western Spirituality. New York: Paulist, 1988.

Aquinas's Shorter Summa. Manchester, NH: Sophia Institute Press, 1993, 2002.

Basic writings of Saint Thomas Aquinas, tr. Anton Charles Pegis. New York: Random House, 1945.

Light of Faith: The Compendium of Theology. Manchester, NH: Sophia Institute Press, 1993.

The Summa theologica, tr. Daniel J. Sullivan. Chicago: Encyclopaedia Britannica, 1955, ©1952.

Nature and grace; selections from the Summa theologica of Thomas Aquinas, tr. A. M. Fairweather. Philadelphia: Westminster, 1954.

Summa theologiae. Latin text and English translation, introductions, notes, appendices, and glossaries. Cambridge: Blackfriars; New York: McGraw-Hill 1964.

Aquinas On being and essence, translated and interpreted by Joseph Bobik. Notre Dame, IN: University of Notre Dame Press, 1965.

An Aquinas reader, ed. Mary T. Clark. New York: Fordham University Press, 1999, ©1972.

Summa theologica. New York: Benziger, 1947–1948.

St. Thomas Aquinas on politics and ethics, tr. Paul E. Sigmund. New York: Norton, 1988.

Treatise on Happiness, tr. John A. Oesterle. Notre Dame, IN: University of Notre Dame Press, 1964, 1983.

Chenu, Marie-Dominique, o.p. *Aquinas and His Role in Theology,* tr. Paul Philibert, o.p. Collegeville: Liturgical Press, 2002.

_____. *Toward Understanding Saint Thomas,* tr. A. M. Landry, o.p., and D. Hughes, o.p. Chicago: Henry Regnery, 1964.

Glenn, Paul J. *A Tour of the Summa.* Saint Louis: Herder, 1963.

O'Meara, Thomas F., o.p. *Thomas Aquinas, Theologian.* Notre Dame, IN: University of Notre Dame Press, 1997.

Weisheipl, James A., o.p. *Friar Thomas D'Aquino: His Life, Thought, and Work.* Garden City, NY: Doubleday, 1974.

Mechthild of Magdeburg (d. 1293)

Mechthild von Magdeburg: Flowing Light of the Divinity, tr. Christiane Mesch Galvani. New York: Garland, 1991.

The Revelations of Mechthild of Magdeburg or The Flowing Light of the Godhead, tr. Lucy Menzies. London: Longmans, Green, 1953.

Meister Eckhart (1260–1329)

Meister Eckhart: The Essential Sermons, Commentaries, Treatises and Defense. Translation and Introduction by Edmund Colledge and Bernard McGinn. New York: Paulist, 1981.

Meister Eckhart: Selected Writings. Translated and edited by Oliver Davies. London: Penguin, 1994.

Meister Eckhart: Teacher and Preacher. Edited and translated by Bernard McGinn with Frank Tobin and Elvira Borgstädt. Preface by Kenneth Northcott. New York: Paulist; London: S.P.C.K., 1987.

Meister Eckhart: Sermons and Treatises, tr. Maurice O'Connell Walshe. 3 vols. Longmead, Shaftesbury, Dorset: Element Books, 1987.

Catherine of Siena (1347–1380)

Catherine of Siena: The Dialogue. Translated and edited by Suzanne Noffke, o.p. New York: Paulist, 1980.

The Letters of Catherine of Siena. Vol. 1. Translated, with Introduction and Notes by Suzanne Noffke, O.P. Binghamton, NY: Medieval and Renaissance Texts and Studies, 1988.

The Letters of Catherine of Siena. Vol. 1. Edited and translated by Suzanne Noffke, O.P. Medieval and Renaissance Texts and Studies. 2d ed. Ithaca: Cornell University Press, 2000.

The Letters of Catherine of Siena. Vol. 2. Edited and translated by Suzanne Noffke, O.P. Medieval and Renaissance Texts and Studies. Tempe: Arizona Center for Medieval and Renaissance Studies, 2001.

The Prayers of Catherine of Siena. Edited and translated by Suzanne Noffke, O.P. New York: Paulist, 1983.

Fra Angelico (John of Fiesole) (1386–1455)

Alce, Venturino, O.P. *"Homilies" of Fra Angelico,* tr. Quentin Lister, O.P. Bologna: Edizioni Studio Domenicano, 1983.

Guillaud, Jacqueline and Maurice. *Fra Angelico: The Light of the Soul: Painting Panels and Frescoes from the Convent of San Marco, Florence.* New York: Clarkson N. Potter, 1986.

Hood, William. *Fra Angelico at San Marco.* New Haven: Yale University Press, 1993.

Morachiello, Paolo. *Fra Angelico: The San Marco Frescoes,* tr. Eleanor Daunt. New York: Thames and Hudson, 1996.

Pope-Hennessy, John Wyndham. *Fra Angelico.* Ithaca, NY: Cornell University Press, 1974.

Spike, John T. *Fra Angelico.* New York: Abbeville Press, 1996.

Antoninus Fierozzi (1389–1459)

Gaughan, William T. *Social Theories of Saint Antoninus from His Summa Theologica.* Catholic University Studies in Sociology 35. Washington, DC: Catholic University of America Press, 1951.

Howard, Peter Francis. *Beyond the Written Word: Preaching and Theology in the Florence of Archbishop Antoninus.* Florence: Leo S. Olschki, 1995.

Supplement to the Liturgy of the Hours for the Order of Preachers: A Draft Translation of the Proprium Officiorum Ordinis Praedicatorum (1982) for Study and Consultation. River Forest, IL: Dominican Liturgical Commission, U.S.A., 1991.

Walker, James B., O.P. The *"Chronicles" of Saint Antoninus: A Study in Historiography.* Catholic University of America Studies in Medieval History 6. Washington, DC: Catholic University of America Press, 1933.

Bartolomé de las Casas (1474–1566)

Bartolomé de las Casas; a selection of his writings. Translated and edited by George W. Sanderlin. New York: Knopf, 1971.

The Devastation of the Indies; a brief account. Translated and edited by Hans Magnus Enzensberger and Michael van Nieuwstadt. New York: Seabury, 1974.

The Diario of Christopher Columbus's First Voyage to America, 1492–1493, tr. Oliver Dunn and James E. Kelley, Jr. Norman, OK: University of Oklahoma Press, 1989.

In defense of the Indians; the defense of the Most Reverend Lord, Don Fray Bartolomé de las Casas, of the Order of Preachers, late Bishop of Chiapa, against the persecutors and slanderers of the peoples of the New World discovered across the seas, tr. Stafford Poole. DeKalb, IL: Northern Illinois University Press, 1974.

Indian Freedom: The Cause of Bartolomé de Las Casas: A Reader, tr. Francis Patrick Sullivan, s.j. Kansas City, MO: Sheed & Ward, 1995.

The Only Way. Edited by Helen Rand Parish. Translated by Francis Patrick Sullivan, s.j. New York: Paulist, 1992.

A Short Account of the Destruction of the Indies, tr. Nigel Griffin. London and New York: Penguin, 1992.

Tears of the Indians, by Bartolomé de las Casas, & The Life of Las Casas, by Sir Arthur Helps. Introduction by Lewis Hanke. Williamstown, MA: J. Lilburne, 1970.

Gutiérrez, Gustavo. *Las Casas: In Search of the Poor of Jesus Christ,* tr. Robert R. Barr. Maryknoll, NY: Orbis, 1993.

Catherine de' Ricci (1522–1589)

Capes, Florence Mary. *St. Catherine de' Ricci: Her Life, Her Letters, Her Community.* London: Burns & Oates, n.d.

Catherine de Ricci. *Selected Letters,* tr. Domenico Di Agresti. Oxford: Dominican Sources, 1985.

_____. *Le Lettre spirituali è familiari di Santa Caterina de' Ricci, Fiorentina,* ed. Cesare Guasti. Prato: Ranieri Guasti, 1861.

Guidi, Fra Filippo, Fiorentino. *Vita della Venerabile Madre Suor Caterina de' Ricci.* Firenze: Sermatelli, 1617.

Sandrini, Fra Domenico Maria. *Vita di Santa Caterina de' Ricci . . . delle Ordine di San-Domenico.* Firenze: Francesco Moücke, 1747.

Serafino, Razzi de' Predicatori. *Vita della Venerabile Madre Suor Caterina de' Ricci, vergine, nobil fiorentina, monaca nel monastero di San-Vincenzio di Prato.* Lucca: Busdraghi, 1594.

Virginio, Vassechi, Cassinese, Bresciano. *Compendio della Vita della beata Caterina de' Ricci, ee., estratto da processi fatti per la sua beatificazione.* Firenze: Paperini, 1733.

Vita di Santa Caterina de' Ricci, cavata dai sommairi dei processi fatti per la sua beatificazione è canonizazione, proposti ed essaminasti nella sagra congregazione de' Riti. Rome: Girolamo Mainardi, 1746.

Martin de Porres (1579–1639)

Cavallini, Giuliana. *St. Martin de Porres, Apostle of Charity,* tr. Caroline Holland. Saint Louis: Herder, 1963.

Fumet, Stanislas. *Life of St. Martin de Porres, Patron Saint of Interracial Justice,* tr. Una Morrissy. Garden City, NY: Doubleday, 1964.

Tarry, Ellen. *Martin de Porres, Saint of the New World.* New York: Vision Books, 1963.

Henri-Dominique Lacordaire (1802–1861)

An Historical Sketch of the Order of St. Dominic: or, A Memorial to the French People. New York: P. O'Shea, 1869.

Conferences of the Rev. Père Lacordaire, delivered in the Cathedral of Nôtre Dame, in Paris, tr. Henry D. Langdon. New York: P. O'Shea, 1870.

Essay on the Re-Establishment in France of the Order of Preachers. Edited by Simon Tugwell, O.P., with an Introduction by André Duval, O.P. Dominican Sources: New Editions in English. Oak Park, IL: Parable; Dublin: Dominican Publications, 1983.

God: Conferences delivered at Nôtre Dame in Paris, tr. Henry D. Langdon. New York: P. O'Shea, 1871.

God and Man. Conferences delivered at Nôtre Dame in Paris. New York: P. O'Shea, 1879.

Jesus Christ. God. God and Man. Conferences delivered at Nôtre Dame in Paris by the Rev. Père Lacordaire, tr. Henry D. Langdon. Manchester: James Robinson; London: Chapman & Hall, 1902.

Letters to Young Men. New York: Benziger, 1905.

Life: Conferences delivered at Toulouse. New York: P. O'Shea, 1875.

Life of Saint Dominic. London: Burns and Oates, 1883.

Political and Social Philosophy. Edited and translated by Denis O'Mahony. London: K. Paul, Trench, Trubner; Saint Louis: Herder, 1924.

Thoughts and Teachings of Lacordaire. London: Art and Book Co., 1902.

Montalembert, Charles Forbes, Comte de. *Memoir of the Abbe Lacordaire.* Authorized Translation. London: R. Bentley, 1863.

Sheppard, Lancelot. *Lacordaire: A Biographical Essay.* New York: Macmillan, 1964.

Rose Hawthorne Lathrop (1851–1926)

Congregation of St. Rose of Lima, Hawthorne, New York, U.S.A. *The Rule of St. Augustine and the Constitutions of the Servants of Relief for Incurable Cancer.* Hawthorne, NY: Congregation of St. Rose of Lima, 1927.

Lathrop, George Parsons. *A Story of Courage; Annals of the Georgetown Convent of the Visitation of the Blessed Virgin Mary.* Boston: Houghton, 1894.

Lathrop, Rose Hawthorne. *Rose Hawthorne Lathrop: Selected Writings,* ed. Diana Culbertson. New York: Paulist, 1993.

_____. *Memories of Hawthorne.* Boston and New York: Houghton Mifflin, 1923.

_____, ed. *Passages From the English Note-Books, of Nathaniel Hawthorne.* Boston: Houghton Mifflin, 1898.

_____, ed. *The Complete Writings of Nathaniel Hawthorne: With an Introduction by His Daughter Mrs. Rose Hawthorne Lathrop: in twenty-two volumes.* Boston: Houghton Mifflin, 1900.

Servants of Relief for Incurable Cancer. *Report of the Servants of Relief for Incurable Cancer.* Hawthorne, NY, 1920–1943.

Georges-Yves Congar (1904–1995)

Called to Life, tr. William Burridge. New York: Crossroad, 1987.

Diversity and Communion, tr. John Bowden. Mystic, CT: Twenty-Third Publications, 1985.

I Believe in the Holy Spirit. Vol. 1: The Holy Spirit in the "Economy," tr. David Smith. New York: Seabury, 1983.

Lay People in the Church, tr. Donald Attwater. Westminster, MD: Newman Press, 1965.

The Mystery of the Temple, tr. Donald Attwater. Westminster, MD: Newman Press, 1962.

Nichols, Aidan, O.P. *Yves Congar.* Wilton, CT: Morehouse-Barlow, 1989.

Edward Schillebeeckx (1914–)

Revelation and Theology. New York: Sheed & Ward, 1967.

Celibacy. New York: Sheed & Ward, 1968.

Christ, the Sacrament of the Encounter with God. New York: Sheed & Ward, 1963.

God Among Us: The Gospel Proclaimed. London: SCM Press, 1983.

God, the Future of Man. New York: Sheed & Ward, 1968.

Man as Man and Believer. New York: Paulist, 1967.

God and Man. New York: Sheed & Ward, 1969.

The Eucharist. New York: Sheed & Ward, 1968.

Mary, Mother of the Redemption. New York: Sheed & Ward, 1964.

The Layman in the Church, and Other Essays. Staten Island, NY: Alba House, 1967.

Vatican II: the Real Achievement. New York: Sheed & Ward, 1968.

Timothy Radcliffe (1945–)

I Call You Friends. London and New York: Continuum, 2001.

Sing a New Song: The Christian Vocation. Springfield, IL: Templegate, 1999.

Seven Last Words. London: Burns and Oates, 2004.